Torah of Sin and Grace

Torah of Sin and Grace

How the Hebrew Prophets Understood the Torah

Michael Tupek

RESOURCE *Publications* · Eugene, Oregon

TORAH OF SIN AND GRACE
How the Hebrew Prophets Understood the Torah

Resource Publications
An Imprint of Wipf and Stock Publishers
199 W. 8th Ave., Suite 3
Eugene, OR 97401
www.wipfandstock.com

ISBN 13: 978-1-62032-506-3
Manufactured in the U.S.A.

Contents

Acknowledgments

I am grateful to Steve Smith for his valuable copyediting service and to Marianne Tavares Pardoe for her encouragement and enthusiasm.

1

The Misunderstood Torah

THE ROLE OF THE first portion of the Hebrew Bible, the Torah, is rather narrowly defined in both Judaism and Christianity so that the full intent of this revered document often goes unappreciated, resulting in a poorer understanding of the grace of God and his redemptive purposes. The purpose of the Torah is not merely being the primary text of the Hebrew existence, nor is it fulfilled in the outgrowth of rabbinic Judaism, nor does it function as a mere legalistic contrast to the grace of the New Testament gospel. Rather, more than the establishment of Israel's covenant and stipulations, *it discloses two profoundly important lessons* throughout its narrative: The serious nature of man's sinfulness and the character of God's saving grace. This lesson of divine grace is the basis upon which unfolds further revelations that disclose a purpose of salvation that will be increasingly realized by the power of God in both Jew and Gentile.

My concern is to provoke an awareness of this problem, since it is reprehensible to misunderstand the precious scriptures that were so graciously given to those who love God and are called according to his purpose. It is also my desire to improve the understanding of the Bible's story by providing a clearer outline of the main events and revelations that progressively develop within its text.

In my writing, I will employ a controlling principle that should have governed all historical Christian theology, which in turn would have prevented the plethora of erroneous teachings found mixed within our Christian heritage today. This principle is the primacy of the Hebrew Bible interpreted in its true Hebrew sense. That is, all theologizing must begin with the earliest revelation, and all religious conceptions must be founded and developed from there. This logical order necessarily involves the strictly Jewish sense of scriptural terms as the controlling sense.

And this was the reverent control of the developed ideas and writings of the Hebrew prophets. They never deviate from the plain sense of the Torah. This should be our reverent control as well. But to ensure this, our safest approach to the Torah is to rightly appreciate the interpretations, insights, and the anxious emphases of the Hebrew prophets, which we find in their writings and recorded prophecies. What the prophets of Yahweh say and teach and reveal is what the Torah really is saying to Yahweh's people. This is how we may know with spiritual certainty that we correctly understand the role of the great scroll of Torah.

It is the Torah of Israel, the first five books comprising the "Pentateuch," which is the foundational revelation. This Torah portion in turn authorizes the subsequent development of revelation and its inscripturation by the divinely appointed means of the former and latter prophets (Deut 18:15–19; Dan 9:6, 10). And then this whole Tanakh, or, "the Law and the Prophets," induces and warrants the final revelation of the Jewish writings of the New Testament (Matt 5:17–18; Acts 3:22–26).

There are also many correlative concerns. I will demonstrate the truth of the inviolable connection between the message of the Hebrew Scriptures and its fulfillment found in the New Testament scriptures. I will demonstrate that the divine grace for man's salvation revealed in the Bible has always been sovereign in character; that is, God gives it only to whom he wills, and he saves only whom he wills. I will demonstrate that this grace is essentially a changed heart toward God, which only God can cause by his initiative, and which produces the kind of faith and love that is acceptable and pleasing to him, securing a right spiritual relationship with him.

2

Method of Study

THE JEWISH (OR SEMITIC) sense of the terminology found utilized within sacred scripture actually employs a universal principle: Those terms and concepts must have definitions that are honestly necessitated by both the biblical context and the ordinary idiomatic usage of that historical situation. As best we can, we need to discern the Hebraic literary conventions of the biblical periods; that is, we need to read scripture in a *plain sense* as an ancient common Hebrew person would have understood it. What did the term mean to the *ordinary person* in that Israelite culture? Throughout the course of this discussion, we shall see, reflected in their own writings, that the prophets read the Pentateuchal narrative in the plain and reasonable sense that the ordinary person would understand. Consequently, they addressed matters of the Torah with a sole concern for the plain and reasonable sense of the passages that would be understood by the common peasant and unsophisticated laborer.

The Hebrew prophets usually addressed all of the people and not just the learned ones; and this is the recognition of the later prophets concerning the purpose of their ministries. They were sent to speak to kings, princes, fathers, and all the people of the land equally (Dan 9:6). The prophets did not abuse the scripture by clever findings of codes and arithmetic, by tedious and convoluted layers of meaning, by fanciful evolutions of myths and fables, by the irrational "omnisignificance" of the texts, or by distracting and blinding "fencings" of the laws. And the subsequent reiterations of the concerns of Torah in the writings of the prophets are all that the people of God need for further authoritative commentary upon it, not the presumptuous authority of the rabbinic sages. If more than the plain-sense readings in the beautiful Hebraic poetry or prose was possible or dutiful, would not we observe it in the handling of the Torah by the inspired prophets themselves?

The simple purpose of divine revelation is ultimately for a personal relationship between God and all redeemed people, not for the intellectual flattery of the elite and sophisticated members of a society. This purpose arises from the unmatched goodness of God, who is no respecter of persons. God created man; therefore, man's first concern is his relationship with his maker. It was God's kindness that in his sovereign providence he caused that the Hebrews would first receive, record, and transmit divine revelation that ensures this relationship, because the Hebrew language is rather simple and straightforward in comparison to the more complicated and eloquent languages of the learned classes of highly–developed civilizations. Again, it was God's kindness to ensure first the spread of common Greek throughout the civilized world, and then to cause both the translation of the Hebrew Bible and later the addition of the New Testament writings to be penned in that accessible tongue.

If scripture interpretation is too abstruse or too difficult to grasp for the ordinary person (from a purely theoretical rather than a moral consideration), then it probably misses the mark for such a purpose of relationship with God. This is ultimately the judgment of Moses, the giver of the laws to the people of Israel, that nothing that he is commanding is "too difficult, or out of reach," supposing they have the willingness to obey it (Deut 30:11–14). Therefore, it is simply not true that, according to the pantheon of sages and rabbis, the Bible is basically cryptic and can only be understood by the skilled and scholarly elite. That the people need teaching in order to accurately see what the plain words are saying is one thing, but to say that the sages need to allure the people to a clever meaning beyond the apprehension of the plain sense is quite another thing. This is sheer abuse of scripture as well as the hearts and minds of the people.

Often, the scriptures are suffused with picturesque metaphors or symbolic language, yet there is still a sense of responsibility toward *discerning the most understandable interpretations* for the ordinary man. Symbolism that is not understood remains useless. This was the attitude of Daniel when he had dreamt of various strange visions. Being agitated by these disturbing premonitions, which were not easily comprehensible, he kept asking the nearby angel as to what they meant (Dan 7:15–16). He was *not satisfied* with simply receiving them, and he did not pretend to understand their sensationalism. He knew there had to be a reasonable explanation for them so as to be *useful for ordinary devotion.* Daniel's attitude regarding divine revelation was very different from some of the rabbis who presumptuously discover ever more removed meanings and unrealistic applications.

It is also not true that the repetition of a commandment or story necessarily and always must have an increased significance to it. Many times, for the sole purpose of emphasis, there are simple repetitions of the same commandments, exhortations, and narratives, without any new or extensible significance. A good example that can refute this ridiculous notion of branching significance of duplicated texts is the repetition of the Ten Commandments. They are repeated in the Torah scroll (Exod 20 and Deut 5). After receiving the original stone tablets on the mountain, Moses had broken them in his anger over the golden calf incident, and then was given another set of tablets engraved with the same ten words (Exod 34:1–28). It is clearly maintained by Yahweh, however, that he rewrote the same words as the first set of tablets. He gave only ten, and not twenty, commandments without any further meaning (Deut 4:13; Deut 10:1–5).

With scripture, we are concerned with specifically Hebraic idiomatic terms, or other relevant ancient Near Eastern terms, found within Hebrew culture during the biblical period. Historically, all lofty or refined spiritual concepts were normally built upon a foundation of mundane concepts that were first understood by the common person. These common terms are the necessary starting points for tracing up to an understanding of more abstract ideas.

But the definition of a refined or religious concept must be anchored and conditioned by the common, ordinary, plain sense of the words used. As an example, we first learn to personally fear some form of ordinary pain or displeasure from someone or something we know on earth, before we are able to understand what it is to fear God in the religious and more spiritual sense. This principle is seen in scripture, speaking of the divine compassion: "Just as a father has compassion on his children, so the Lord has compassion on those who fear him" (Ps 103:13); and again, "I will spare them as a man spares his own son who serves him" (Mal 3:17). This ordinary sense must be reasonably applied and not wildly forced. Ultimately, only the influence of the Spirit of God upon a heart resulting in thoroughgoing honesty will ensure such a practice.

Now, every sentence, statement, and passage has an essential meaning or message that is inspired by the Spirit of God, but verbalized by the influence of the Spirit upon the individual personality of the prophet speaking or writing. This would have taken place at the time of the prophet's historical activity, and it is this recorded communication that has become our divinely inspired scripture. The fidelity of the divine revelation would have been ensured by the Spirit influencing the prophet and the possible redactors of these sacred communications, up until the providential closing of the canon of scripture.

The essential meaning may be safely paraphrased by those who have the ability to expound the scriptures to others, in all ages, even as the priests and Levites taught the people (Neh 8:7; Mal 2:7). They surely explained the word of God with reasonable re-phrasing, and did not slavishly repeat it *verbatim*. This can be seen when we read of the summaries of the Torah events or requirements mentioned by the prophets (Hos 12:2–4; Amos 3:2; Mic 6:8).

But there is an important control during this exercise of teaching the word. It is the boundary comprised of each and all of the inspired terms relevant to a contextual concept, including their legitimate senses, which are found in a text. The essence of a text is, as it were, shaped by all of the words employed in the verses of both the immediate and wider contexts. Should one of the words be ignored, or taken out of context, or perverted to mean something unregulated by the contextual usage, the shape then becomes distorted—we no longer have the meaning originally intended by the Spirit, but rather an imaginary notion devoid of spiritual power and authority. That is, an untrue condition will never be maintained in divine providence as reality, and the Holy Spirit's power will never influence a wrong characterization of godliness.

Scriptural revelation is only communicated by the Hebrew prophets (Deut 18:15; Dan 9:6, 10; Amos 3:7) and through no other; neither Jewish rabbi nor Christian minister. There is no post-biblical tradition worthy of the reverence that is to be accorded to the Bible. In the New Testament, the Apostle Peter commands the careful consideration of the words of the Hebrew prophets as the distinctive duty of those who would be the followers and recipients of the redemption of the Messiah, Jesus (2 Pet 3:2). More than this, he commends such careful consideration as being the surest means to understanding the core message of redemptive history, as sure as the indisputable help that the coming of the dawn is to those who need the light of the bright sun to live by (2 Pet 1:19). God is clear and emphatic that there should be no adding to, or taking away from, the given corpus of divine revelation (Deut 4:2; Deut 12:32; Prov 30:6).

Despite the sanctity and the injunctions of scripture, the rabbis transgress and have stretched the definition of "Torah" to include the records of the post-biblical verbal interactions of Jewish scholars throughout all the ages since the closing of the canon. They are often dismissive of their own Hebrew grammar, suspend the reasonable interpretation of the Tanakh, and substitute imaginary possibilities of the isolated letters, words, and distant connections of similar terms, which do violence to the contextual sense. They have persistently added to the revelation of Yahweh by the endless accretions of sayings and comments of the Jewish sages in the form of their revered traditions and Talmud. Because of the hardness of their heart and the deadness of their current exilic religion, some of Judaism are discontented with the canon of revealed scripture, not being able to spiritually appreciate the actual riches of the Bible, and have pursued a more titillating religion, feeding on the wild fantasies of Kabbalism and esoteric codes and clues of the Hebrew text.

The "Oral Torah" is a patent absurdity that commits logical suicide. Supposedly, the reason for the oral law is to safely explain the written law, but this is ridiculous because it has been written down by the rabbis in about 200 CE, proving that all of the supposed oral tradition could have been written down simultaneously with the written law. This fact in turn proves that if there was a need for an explicative law to safely teach the written law, it could have been written down alongside the principal law. In other words, whatever was needed to be heard and observed at Sinai had in fact been written down completely. There is no scriptural passage in the Torah narrative, nor anywhere else in the Tanakh for that matter, that honestly records such a significant event as the coetaneous dispensing of both of these supposed kinds of laws by Moses at Sinai. We only read of the words or laws being written down for the sake of observation and posterity, and all the revelation of God was considered as a "book" (Exod 24:3–4; Exod 34:27; Deut 31:9; Josh 1:7–8; Josh 8:34).

The scriptures declare that everything that Moses commanded was written and there was nothing left unwritten, which refutes the giving of an oral law at that same time (Josh 8:35). In Hosea, Yahweh protested to sinful Israel that he had caused to be written his many instructions for their religious worship, which they regarded as strange things due to their lack of love for him, but there is no suggestion that the people were disrespectful to a supposed oral tradition of his laws (Hos 8:12). Furthermore, several hundred years later, when Judah fell into a general apostasy by neglecting the covenant and will of God as revealed in the Torah, the people of Judah only became aware of their sinful backsliding when a copy of the written law was found and read (2 Kgs 22:8–13), thereby disproving the supposed existence of an unbroken oral tradition safeguarding the written will of God.

If there had been a thriving oral tradition, the people would not need to have discovered a written copy of Torah to become aware of the violated covenant. Again, why would Ezra the scribe need to read the book of the law of Moses to "those who could understand" what he had read when there was supposedly an unbroken oral tradition always available to safely explain the law of Moses (Neh 8:1–3)?

It is also important to realize in our examination of the Hebrew Bible that the prophets themselves do not isolate letters and words, ripping them from their context, and then offer teachings or build doctrines upon them. Further, they do not ever consult a supposed oral tradition but refer to the scriptures as written scrolls (Dan 9:2, 11). These settled practices of rabbinic Judaism are not supported by the later authors of sacred scripture themselves as they never handle the previous revelation of the Torah as do the rabbis. Finally, it was understood in the biblical period that when there was no prophet, there was no authoritative word to be revered in the sense that it was inspired by the Spirit of God (Deut 18:20; Ps 74:9).

Many Christians also handle the Bible fraudulently when they often force a preconceived Western definition of particular terms upon the Hebrew text while failing to honor the Hebrew Scriptures by carefully researching the historical-grammatical Jewish sense of terms and their employment by the Hebrew authors. For example, "day" does not always mean a twenty-four-hour period of time. There is also a tendency to read into the Hebrew Scriptures some of the fully disclosed teachings of the New Testament more than is honestly warranted, such as that the actual person of "Jesus" yet to come was known to certain prophets of old. Or, Christians can develop teachings from New Testament passages without considering how they are qualified by the Old Testament's disclosures.

Many Christians also abuse the Bible in the same manner as the Jews by constructing doctrines upon rather selective portions of the scriptures, resulting in textual dishonesty and imbalanced, fanciful, and distorted theologies. They focus on favorable passages while they disregard, distort, or minimize those passages that they dislike or find hard to bear, and then develop customized belief systems. This is nothing less than dishonesty with the word of truth.

There is also the persistent attack of modern criticism upon the divine inspiration and general historicity of the Bible, by the mainly non-evangelical academia, who basically describe the scriptures as a hodge-podge of uninspired works of fiction by authors and redactors who are ultimately motivated by base human agendas. But this is only the natural result of scholars who are unrenewed by the Spirit of God themselves and who cannot help but be driven in their assessments by categories of mere human existence and not the gifted apprehension that comes by grace. All that they know are fleshly ways of behavior and, therefore, that is all that they can assign to the formation of the scriptures.

If mankind is generally found to be dishonest, self-seeking, and politically ambitious, then the writers of scripture must have been also! But unbelief always seeks its own havens and environs.

3

Legitimate Theology Is Hebraic

ALL LEGITIMATE CHRISTIAN THEOLOGY is Hebraic in origin and sense, because salvation is from the Jews; therefore, the revealed will of God must of necessity be conveyed through their culture. The Hebrews called by God, the Jews, are a "holy seed" (Ezra 9:2) established for his glory to be reflected in them both in salvation and holiness (Deut 4:6–8). It is to Israel that God has directly given his words and laws, and to no other nation (Ps 147:19–20). To the Israelites were given the glory and the covenants, and it is through their seed that the Messiah was promised (Rom 9:4–5). Therefore all Hebrew-Christian theology must, from a logical standpoint and the demand of the order of the historical progress of divine revelation, begin with the roots of revelatory ideas—which were, in fact, granted to the Hebrews alone. These ideas must then inform the legitimate branching of the progressive development of divine revelation within the biblical period of Israel's history.

In other words, the Torah's contents, despite the date of its final composition, were the principal body of revelation and the beginnings of the redemptive acts of God. The authorized prophets developed their ideas and messages from the seminal conceptions, statements, narratives, declarations, inferences, and laws of these original writings. Again, even if it should be successfully demonstrated that the Pentateuch includes the work of later redactors (while yet maintaining the divine inspiration and essential historicity of the canonical form), this body of work still logically contains the beginnings of the redemptive activities of God.

It is here that we find not only the distant past of humanity's origins, written in the poetic craft of the early writers, but we observe the origins of mankind's fall and the gracious initiative of the living God in bringing people near to him in a restored relationship through the giving of the glorious provisions of revelation, atonement, and laws for his honor. Therefore, the legitimate theology that should result from such a governed procedure is a purely Hebraic theology uninfluenced in its essential message by Greco-Roman philosophy or pagan conceptions. This Hebraic understanding of scripture is what operated in the minds of Jesus and his disciples, and which should be the goal of our theological strivings as well. Otherwise, we hold to a questionable theology, much of which is imaginary. We will then be in danger of committing the sin of adding to, or taking away from, the words that God has given us (Deut 4:2; Deut 12:32; Deut 29:29; Prov 30:6; Rev 22:18–19).

For evangelical Christians, it is critically important that we disabuse ourselves of the subtle gentile-supremacy attitude that has conditioned the church for centuries. We must retrain our minds to be profoundly conscious of the priceless mercy that Yahweh had eventually extended to the gentile nations beyond the calling of the Hebrews, in providing salvation from sin and estrangement. This redemptive purpose was first and only given to the Hebrews, but then in the course of time it was brought to the nations. Therefore, unless gentile believers are in some measure struck with horror that they might have been justly left to their pagan darkness had not God willed to include all the nations, they do not fully appreciate the grace that saves, and will go about their Christian walk with shameful stupidity, robbing God of glory!

The Jews named this beginning portion of divine revelation from a term that is used by God and Moses to designate the essential nature of its contents. It was called the Torah תורה. This word means "instruction." It denotes any message communicated by God regarding his will and man's salvation for our authoritative knowledge.

This can be ascertained through the parallelism of Hebrew poetry as seen, for example, in Micah 4:2, "for from Zion will go forth the law, even the word of the Lord from Jerusalem." It does not mean "law" in the legal sense of rule as most versions have it, even though the Septuagint translators and the Greek New Testament writers termed it "the Law," using the Greek word νομος, indicating the prominence of its mandatory character. Laws are prominently instructed within this book, and so this term was used because God's commandments were given for the purpose of informing the people of Israel how to fear and love him. But the commandments, laws, statutes, and judgments were to be taught to the people, and each generation was to teach these to their offspring (Deut 4:1, 5, 9–10; Deut 6:7; Deut 11:18–19).

But much more than laws was given in this body of instruction. It also comprised the narrative of God's interactions with his people, such as his saving activities toward them (consisting of deliverances and blessings) and his reprobation of them for their failures of covenant stipulations (consisting of displeasures and judgments). This is seen within the testimony of the Torah as to the literary activity of Moses himself, consisting of narrative, legislature, and poetry. His writings, no doubt, formed the core text upon which later authors or redactors developed the canonical form of the Pentateuch (Exod 17:14; Exod 24:4; Exod 34:27–28; Num 33:2; Deut 31:22).

4

The Wider Role of the Torah in the Bible

THE BIBLE'S OWN VIEW of the Torah's overarching purposes can be seen by considering the *usage of the Bible writers* themselves. In contradistinction to the rabbinic tradition formulated during the Second Temple period, the view of the writers of scripture is rather different and much broader in scope. That is, the traditional Jewish view of the Torah is the narrow regard of this corpus as the supreme embodiment of the divine laws for God's covenant and worship. And this is true and correct insofar as it contains the revelatory prescription for holiness and covenant fidelity, in that particular distinctive manner commanded of Israel, so they could serve and worship the living God. But this view is too narrow. In fact, so poor can the Jewish regard of the Torah be, that it has been shamefully epitomized by the fourth century sage Rabbi Yitzhak, who stated that little would have been lost if the Torah had been started in the middle of Exodus, where the commandments begin, because the law is the crux of this revelation!

There is a tremendous difference between formal obedience that is *secretly driven by fear,* and the personal relationship that is *sustained by love.* A relationship of enjoyable worship and affectionate attachment to Yahweh is the goal of the Torah, not mere obedience to laws and rituals. When the biblical writers discuss or refer to the Torah, it is with a regard to this corpus as having a much broader purpose beyond the revealed moral will of God—more than a legal code for holiness. They see it also as an embodiment of *profound initial manifestations* having primarily a didactive and revelatory character. In fact, the biblical writers regard it as the *principal record* of the divine interventions and interactions that is to be *dutifully consulted,* which reveals the nature of man's sin and the nature of God's grace in response to this condition.

The Torah is seen as the unveiling of the beginnings of God's redemptive purposes for all mankind through the election of the Hebrews. It is revered as the norm and controlling doctrinal standard, not only of the moral will of God that it necessarily contains concerning the divine covenant, but also of the fearful principle of sin and the sovereign character of God's grace in redemption.

When we carefully examine the Pentateuchal narrative and then review and compare the later biblical period's *references to this narrative,* it becomes apparent what the Holy Spirit's *principal concerns* really are. We see the primary intent of this corpus as indeed *torah,* that of teaching important truths for the sake of rightly appreciating what God is revealing to us about himself and about all of mankind, and not merely "Torah" delimited to the culture of the Jews. We can see this confirmed by the frequency and kinds of *recalled events,* proving what were the real concerns that God had his prophets address to the people. The critical importance of this observation between the Torah document and the particular regard of the later prophets must not be overlooked, and can be demonstrated as follows:

First, the beginnings of the divine redemptive history in broad outlines entail man's innocence at creation, the fall of man, the divine promise of salvation through a man, the calling of Abraham, the promises of the covenant, the Hebrew enslavement, the calling of Moses and deliverance through him, the giving of the law at Sinai, the failure of Israel to keep covenant, the punitive wandering in the desert, the termination of the wilderness generation, and then the completion of Moses' service (Genesis through Deuteronomy). In general terms, it is the era of Moses that is principally recorded. Through these events, God reveals the profound truths of the real power of sin seen in the failure of Israel and the fearful necessity of divine intervention for salvation, which Yahweh disclosed and had given in selective instances.

Even before the Israelites had crossed into the Promised Land, Moses was compelled to recount the history of Israel since the exodus and the establishment of the national covenant up until that point. But what was his purpose in doing so? It was to exhort the people to love and obey Yahweh who had so magnificently redeemed them and in lovingkindness had given his covenant of grace to be their God—and they were to be his sons and daughters by the exercise of faith and love in God. The reiteration of the laws was but a part of Moses' speech. The main concern was to admonish and persuade the people to appreciate the grace that Yahweh had shown them and to live accordingly.

God's grace shown in his redemptive acts for Israel should have induced loving reliance and devotion toward him, a relationship of faith and honor, as is indicated by Yahweh's complaint of the people, "How long will this people spurn me? And how long will they not believe in me, despite all the signs which I have performed in their midst?" אשׁר עשׁיתי בקרבו עד־אנה לא־יאמינו בי בכל האתות (Num 14:11). The term for believe אמן characteristically denotes something reliable, and so would involve a loving reliance in God's revealed character, as demonstrated by Abraham who is said to have made himself rely upon Yahweh והאמן ביהוה (Gen 15:6).

This exhortation to faith and love in Yahweh is seen in many verses of Moses' farewell address (Deut 1:29–33; Deut 8:1–6; Deut 29:1–9; Deut 32:5–14). This was the goal of God's salvation of Israel, but it was not achieved with them. It is important to realize that these recorded events that make up the Pentateuchal narrative were the *actual concern and burden* of the author(s) of these documents, composed under the inspiration of the Spirit of God. All of these events, not just the legal codes, were the real intention of the composer(s) of this great scroll.

An important corollary to this observation is the evidential historicity of the Torah document. The sheer facts that the Pentateuchal narrative entails include not only the unheard of account of a purely theocentric origin for the establishment of the Israelites as a covenanted society with absolutely no credit to the Hebrews themselves, but also the sad and shameful conclusion of that very people's failure to be a respectable covenant-keeping nation!

Can it be seriously contemplated, according to modern criticism, that this people group would fabricate the glorious tale of their God, who lovingly rescued them from slavery and oppression because of covenantal promise to their patriarchs and gave them the highest ethical standards, including the condemnation of false testimony? Would they then continue the tale with their inability to love their God in return, as demonstrated in appalling rebellions and covenant-breaking, as the final conclusion to the most important document of their existence? And would this very tale be faithfully maintained throughout this people's collective memory, copying it as their sacred scriptures, generation after generation, with the damning recollections and rebukes through the noble office of Prophetism? Then ultimately, would they close the developed canon of Hebrew

Scriptures with yet renewed and continued rebellions and covenant-breaking? No! Only a people who had been really dealt with, as described in the scriptures, and the honesty of the sanctified few prophets, can possibly wish to maintain such a disappointing story of their origins.

Second, the later prophets and psalmists then reference many of the same significant events and divine interactions from these beginning experiences of Israel with her gracious God as recorded during this earlier biblical period. But it is not merely the law that they recall in exhorting Israel to their duty. They also emphatically point out the great grace and mercy that God had shown his redeemed people, and the subsequent rebellion and failure of his people to love him in return. Along with these events they tell of God's recurring covenantal lovingkindness and compassion on their afflictions in delivering and forgiving them upon repentance, and their recurring backslidings into sin and disloyalty to him. The later prophets also perceive and expand upon the truth already revealed to Moses, that a supernatural change of the heart is absolutely and fearfully necessary in order to realize the ideal of covenant love and loyalty to God. Some notable examples are:

Nehemiah

In Nehemiah 9:5–37, we have recorded the Jewish leaders' long confession of Israel's guilt before God. Again, the people are *compelled to recount* the sinful failures of Israel, not only from the relatively recent backslidings of the divided nation of Israel and Judah (v 32) but also including the initial covenant violations of the Mosaic era recorded in the Torah (vv 16–21) up through the conquest and settlement of the land of Canaan (vv 22–31).

These exilic returnees see and consider the significance of the narrative backbone of the Torah, which tells of the redemptive acts of Yahweh in the gracious giving of his covenant and laws to the descendants of Abraham (vv 7–15), and of Israel's recurring sinful failing of the covenant (vv 16–17, 26, 28–30, 34–35), and of the contrasting steadfastness of Yahweh's covenant lovingkindness toward them—both in the form of forgiveness and of preserving a remnant of this called race (vv 17, 19–25, 27–28, 30–31, 33).

It is very telling that they repeat the general indictment of the Song of Moses in that Israel "ate and grew fat" on God's bounty, and then became arrogant and rebellious toward God (vv 25–26; see Deut 32:15).

They understand that not only was God good and gracious in giving his praiseworthy laws to Israel, but also that they should be persuaded to profound love and loyalty to God because of the great mercy and favor that he lavished upon them (vv 17, 35).

Psalm 44

This *maskil* shows the purpose of the Torah is largely the instruction of the salvation history of Israel, which was learned from the Hebrew fathers recounting the events of the Torah. In particular, it reveals the significant events of Israel's supernatural conquest of the land of Canaan by the favor of God, in order to "plant" his people according to his gracious covenant. And then the psalm mentions the more recent experiences of Israel's affliction and defeat as a nation before her enemies. Finally, there is the pleading for God's help by the godly of the land.

Contrary to rabbinic practice, the psalmists' perception of the most important instruction of the Torah is not the collection of *mitzvot* (conventional Jewish commandments) but the factual history of the redemptive grace of Yahweh toward this people and the necessary call to express in turn the appropriate faith and love toward God according his prescribed will. What the godly psalmists have learned from the fathers' teaching of Torah is the favor of God in establishing the people of Israel and settling them in the land of Canaan for the sake of a covenanted relationship with them. It was not their military abilities that accomplished this national victory (vv 1–3). And then there is the commanded appropriate response of trust and gratitude in keeping covenant with Yahweh, expressed according to "the way" revealed in the Torah (vv 4–8, 17–18).

In this psalm, there is the curious absence of particular sins as being the provocation of God's punishment of the people. There are always the ordinary sinful failings of any man, but it is here protested distinctly that there is no consciousness of rebellion or deviation from the service of God to especially merit his chastisements. However, this does demonstrate that the mere keeping of the *mitzvot* is not the sum purpose of the Torah. There is the deeper spiritual concern of having a heart toward God which has "not dealt falsely with his covenant," and "has not turned back," nor "deviated from his way," because "he knows the secrets of the heart" (vv 17–18, 20–21). This is undoubtedly protested against the known background of the history of the general failings of Israel as a called people recorded in the Torah.

The godly psalmists know that they themselves loved God for his redemptive grace, and felt that they had the genuine faith and devotion that his revelation had demanded. In the end, they continued to look to the "lovingkindness" of God for their help, and not the proud confidence of keeping the letter of the law (v 26). Yes, there was a holy confidence in having kept the way of God (Ps 17:3–5; Ps 18:20–24), but there was also the more profound lesson of reliance on the sheer grace of God for salvation, rather than a supposed meritorious fastidiousness of keeping *mitzvot*.

Psalm 78

The songs of Asaph, a pious lover of God, are some of the most significant in their recollections of the earlier biblical history of God's redemptive acts with Israel. In Psalm 78, Asaph begins his psalm with a plea to hear his teaching תורה (vv 1–2). He recognizes the didactic role of the Torah's narrative, from which he presupposes and recalls. He demonstrates that the Torah teaches not only the legal codes but also such things as the praises of God's grace and his wondrous works (vv 3–8). And he will continuously mention the disposition of the heart of the people of Israel, and also of David's their great pious king (vv 8, 18, 37, 72). Asaph asserts that the glorious grace of Yahweh toward Israel should be remembered as well as the law kept, and that the people should have been persuaded by these acts of redemption to believe the words of God and to apply themselves to wholehearted trust and loyalty to his covenant (vv 7, 11, 22, 32, 42–43).

Asaph will recount the narrative portions that contain God's redemptive acts and the shameful treacheries of Israel, from the earlier biblical period, as the great instructive lessons of these scrolls (vv 9–64). Then finally, in contrast to the disappointing failures of Israel due to their lack of a right heart toward Yahweh, he will mention the sovereign resolve of God to elect his own choice of a sanctuary site, his own choice of the tribe through which he will rule his people, and his own choice of a king (David) for them (vv 65–72) —all which requires the supernatural power of God to bring about and which would not have occurred passively. It only appeared as if God had no power in the previous historical matters, but then "the Lord awoke as if from sleep" (v 65). He then resolved, for the glory of his inheritance (v 71), to put forth his power in accomplishing what he will have done, including the necessary integrity of heart that David needed to shepherd his people successfully (v 72).

Psalm 102

In this psalm there is the poignant prayer of a godly man crying to God for compassion and deliverance from some oppressive affliction. He obviously loves God and trusts in both his historical and declared grace toward the Hebrew people, both nationally and individually. We know that he has genuine spiritual love for God because he reveres the revealed character and the covenanted grace toward Israel. That is, he reveres his "name" (v 21) as both holy and gracious (vv 19–20), as well as the glory of both his works in creation (v 25) and the divine establishment and concerns for "Zion" (vv 13–16). He also proves his love because he recognizes the divine chastisements (vv 9–10, 24), and seeks compassion ultimately from him by praying and trusting in his revealed word (vv 1–2, 13).

But most importantly for my argument are the statements in one particular portion (vv 18–22), where we have the significant principle demonstrated—that scripture is written specifically *to recount* the grace of God toward his redeemed people, and for the inducement of gratitude and holy living in response to his kindness. It is asserted in verse 18, "This will be written for the generation to come; that a people yet to be created may praise the Lord" תכתב זאת לדור אחרון ועם נברא יהלל־יה. It is immaterial whether the psalmist is referring to the foundational deliverance of the Hebrew slaves in Egypt, or a more recent experience of the nation. The principle stands. Scripture is for the *memorializing* (vv 12, 21) the redemptive acts of God and the *inducement* of loving devotion in response to this grace. It is not for the delimited and sterile purpose of enumerating a *halakhic formula of mitzvot*.

Psalm 105

This psalm emphasizes the teaching of the Torah in stating the marvelous grace and works on behalf of the Hebrew Patriarchs and the nation of Israel. These things are to be *recalled* from the inspired scroll, and the expected response is the praise, gratitude, and righteous devotion commanded by God (vv 1–6, 45). The rest of this psalm is a *salvation history* of significant events recorded in the Torah and briefly recounted (vv 7–44). The most important things that are praised by this psalmist are the grace and faithfulness of Yahweh concerning the words, promises, and covenant given to the Patriarchs and their descendants as the basis of his redemption granted to the Israelites (vv 7–13, 42–44). According to this inspired psalmist, the purpose of the Torah is largely the historical teaching of God's grace shown in the electing redemption of the Hebrews (vv 5, 8–44), and his faithfulness in keeping his word to them. It then calls for the appropriate response of loving reliance and holiness of life (vv 1–5, 45).

Again, we see that the Torah is not regarded by the biblical servant as a mere catalog of rules, nor are stringent formulaic *mitzvot* ever mentioned as that which God seeks from those who worship him. To be sure, the teaching of Torah comprises the laws for righteous living and religious duty prescribed for the people of Israel especially. But these commandments were not for meriting the divine approval but for *ensuring and proving the correct response of love.* What is also clearly demonstrated in this psalm is the fact that Israel's experience of grace and her calling as a holy people *derive from their ancestral relationship with Abraham,* and not their relationship with Moses (vv 6, 9, 42). Israel's very basis for existence is rooted in the Abrahamic covenant (vv 8–12; see Isa 41:8) and is actually conditioned and sustained by that event, so that even if the national covenant with Moses is divinely altered (as we shall see that it was), the foundational covenant is constant.

Psalm 106

This psalm emphasizes the rebelliousness of the nation of Israel despite the magnificent grace shown to the Hebrew people, which is unashamedly recorded within the historical account of the redemption and the establishment of a divinely blessed relationship with Yahweh, written honestly into the scroll of the Torah. Of course, the psalm is written by a man who truly loves and reveres God and clearly demonstrates that his own spirit has been transformed by the supernatural grace of the Holy Spirit. Therefore, we see exemplified the correct religious feelings toward Yahweh and which are also wished for the people of Israel for whom he naturally writes. He begins with the gratitude owed for God's grace (vv

1–5) given to those of the people who prove their spiritual and honest appreciation for it. This is not all of Israel but to those "who keep justice" and "who practice righteousness at all times" (v 3).

There is a close connection between the divine "goodness," "loving-kindness," and "mighty deeds" of the Mosaic era, and the "blessedness" of those who did now live for the sake of God's honor. Grace begins with granted goodness, deliverance, and the establishment of covenantal relationship, and the appropriate response is the soul of the covenanted believer *steered by God's honor*. The believer's spirit will be so naturally bent toward the valuation and craving for the lovingkindness of God that he will honestly seek for the continued participation in, and enjoyment of, divine favor toward those who belong to him. This very participation in the favor granted to those who belong to God will be, in turn, the very reason the believer feels he has grounds for glorying in God (vv 4–5). Sadly, the majority of this psalm is the *indictment* of Israel's failure to be the covenanted people of God. Both the wilderness generation and the following formative national generations are especially in the psalmist's mind for the confession of sinful rebellions, despite the initial and continued favor of Yahweh toward the people (vv 6–46).

Very clearly, we see several important spiritual truths concerning the religious experience of the Israelites:

1. That God often delivered them from troubles "for his name's sake" (v 8) and not their righteousness, and so Israel has not merited their continued status as the people of God's choice.

2. They did not have the faith and gratitude that God deserved (vv 13, 21, 24), and so they proved themselves just as evil as the unredeemed heathen around them (vv 40–41).

3. That the mediation of a godly man could be accepted in obtaining the mercy of God toward the people (vv 23, 30).

4. That Israel, despite the dishonest flattery of the rabbis in the Talmud, so failed to be the people that God desired to redeem that he would have destroyed them (vv 23, 26–27, 40–41).

5. That they did not spiritually appreciate the mighty works of God because they were spiritually unchanged, which is why they did not trust God nor lovingly obey him in order to be his covenanted people (vv 7, 13, 21–22, 24; see Deut 29:2–8; Ps 95:9; Heb 3:9).

Isaiah

The great book of Isaiah will be briefly considered here. It does not matter whether there were two or more hands in the writing of this collection of prophecies since the canonical book is the intended scripture that God, in his providence, has granted his people for their salvation. It is through the observations of Isaiah that we hear some of the strongest condemnation of the hypocrisies of the general populace of Judah and Jerusalem concerning the falsehood of their religion before God.

With the Torah as the appropriate basis, Yahweh's judgments toward the covenant people focus on the significant facts of their failure to serve him with love and devotion from the heart for his grace toward them since their establishment as the privileged possession of God. The *indictment* is clear that, ever since their beginnings, they have walked a course of religious hypocrisy and idolatries, believing that they did well because of the performance of external rituals based upon the bare letter of the Law as taught by spiritually-dead leaders (Isa 1:10–17; Isa 29:13; Isa 48:1–2; Isa 66:3–4).

Again, with the Torah as the basis, God condemns the people of Judah and Jerusalem because of their ingratitude for his grace toward them in redeeming them and making them a holy people with great and glorious teachings תורה and ethics (Isa 42:21; see Deut 4:7–8, 32–40). And stressing the words of Moses, God condemns the people for their inability to spiritually appreciate the miraculous things that he had done for them (Isa 42:18–25; see Deut 29:4).

A significant and disturbing complaint is that of Israel's attitude of *spurning* both Yahweh himself and, of course, the Servant who spoke the truth in his name, as the Torah clearly charges (Isa 1:4; Isa 5:24; Isa 49:7; Isa 53:3; see Deut 31:20; Deut 32:15). In this regard, the prophet has a different attitude, in that he recalls and rejoices in God's ancient mercies toward them as a people; and he also recognizes the compassion of God toward them despite their rebellions (Isa 63:7–14). He specifically points out that "the days of old, of Moses" were recalled, and the miraculous interventions and the peace granted for them (Isa 63:10–14). He continues with a yearning for similar "mighty deeds" that God would perform for the sake of the people, who were so favored because of grace toward Abraham and Jacob, as recorded in the Torah (Isa 63:15—64:12).

The prophet *alludes to the judgment of Moses* in declaring that God had not given to Israel the "eyes to see," nor the "ears to hear," nor the "heart to know" his salvation spiritually. But he also adds that neither has anyone spiritually seen the amazing display of loyal love that God shows for the ones who appreciate his favor, for those who love him with an internal love, "who wait for him," "who rejoice in doing righteousness," and "who remembers him in his ways" (Isa 64:4–5). Only Israel has *experienced the reality of a living, helping, and blessing god,* despite the claims of the heathen nations around her. But there are two important correlative elements to this statement of Isaiah: The reality of Yahweh and his mighty power, and the reality of a people who are glad to serve him.

There is then a deeper meaning enunciated here, and which is perceived by the Apostle Paul: The *exclusivity* of the experience of divine intimacy in his grace and help (1 Cor 2:6–16). That is, only those who have been changed by the Spirit will ever really know and spiritually appreciate the closeness of God's heart toward them.

The prophet also writes out the concurring general indictment by God as it was found in the Torah, that his covenanted people had been *a shameful failure* (Isa 65:1–7). It is not the details and precision of the performance of the rituals and ceremonies that he wishes to discuss—it is the grace and goodness given to Israel that is noticed from the Torah.

Again, with the Torah as basis, God condemns them for failing to spiritually know and believe in him alone, since he had graciously demonstrated to them that he is the only true and saving God that they should fear (Isa 43:8–13; see Exod 18:9–11; Exod 19:9; Deut 4:35; Deut 6:4, 13–15; Deut 10:14–15, 20–22). God did not care how well the ritual commandments were executed beyond the Torah's general guidelines, which could be performed with the reasonable care and latitude that accompanies spiritual love for God. We never read of God complaining of the worshiper's inexactitude about the *mitzvot,* as the rabbis have expressed anxiety about. What God did care about was that there would be internal love along with the external offerings.

It is important to understand that Isaiah recognizes the disclosure of the spiritual fact found in the Torah that when God, in his sovereignty, leaves a people to the *sway* of their sinful nature, or "hardens their heart," then the people will inevitably be *indisposed to love or obey him* (Isa 63:17; see Exod 4:21; Exod 7:3; Deut 2:30; Deut 29:4; Ps 81:12). This is one of the core truths revealed through the Torah narrative. Mankind is only and always evil in their fallen nature, and cannot seek or love God in truth. And God will have his redeemed people know this—he will be *desperately needed* and glorified for his grace in their lives.

God also has the prophet express his profound complaint that he had *made himself available* as a savior and a caring God to Israel but that they had only returned infidelity in the covenant relationship (Isa 65:1–7). The Hebrews in Egypt did indeed groan for deliverance, but they did not seek Yahweh for his sake (Exod 2:23; Exod 6:2–9; see Ps 14:2). It was Yahweh's initiating grace that destined them for deliverance and favor. This in turn underscores the other core teaching of the Torah, that only by the influence of God's Spirit can anyone truly seek and love him. So then, the book of Isaiah concurs with the scroll of Moses that Israel was a sinful failure. Isaiah also concurs with Moses that only the influence of the Spirit of God upon the heart would produce the internal love and devotion that God required and deserved (Isa 11:2; Isa 32:15–17; Isa 44:3–5; Isa 54:13–14; Isa 59:21; Isa 63:11).

Jeremiah and Ezekiel

Both of these important prophetic books demonstrate very telling conclusions drawn from the Torah. God pointedly expresses through Jeremiah that his people had disobeyed and had broken the covenant; therefore, he had brought on them the curse threatened within the Torah revelation (Jer 11:1–10; see Deut 29:12). Consequently, both Jeremiah and Ezekiel see that the initial desert covenant that God established with the people of Israel after their deliverance from Egypt was *faulty*, not because of inherently poor design but because *it consisted of a mere external calling.* Jeremiah concurs in his assessment of the old desert covenant with the bare facts of the Torah. The Mosaic redemption preached to Israel's conscience only and demanded an obedience motivated by an outward demonstration of God's power in circumstantial deliverance and earthly blessedness, and fearful wrath threatened for disobedience. Still, despite the kindness of God in thoroughly teaching the people of his instruction for covenant blessedness, Israel and Judah are said, in general terms, to have only turned their back to Yahweh since their calling at Sinai (Jer 32:30–35).

This covenant, therefore, failed in that it did not produce true godliness and loyalty to Yahweh from the heart. Jeremiah announces that there will be a *new covenant implemented by God* that will be effected by his Holy Spirit transforming the hearts of those who will be redeemed (Jer 31:31–34). There is an immense difference, such as there is between death and life, between the external calling of the Sinaitic covenant and the internal calling of the New Covenant that God has willed to make with the house of Israel and the house of Judah.

The faultiness of the Sinai covenant is seen in several ways:

1. It is proven by the *manner* of Israel's redemption under Moses, denoted by the phrase that God employs: "I took them by the hand to bring them out of the land of Egypt" (Jer 31:32);

2. It is proven by the implication of the *necessity* of a "new covenant" ברית חדשה (Jer 31:31);

3. It is proven by the *supernatural character* of the New Covenant, in the provision of the law being put within the people, written on the heart, and the possession of real personal knowledge of Yahweh (Jer 31:33–34).

It is supernatural in that God is not waiting futilely upon Israel's inability to love him. But rather, he will cause his people to love him truly and certainly by means of a supernatural change of their heart's disposition (Jer 32:39–40). Ezekiel also prophesies according to the backdrop of the Torah narrative. He expresses essentially these same convictions—the failure of the people under the old covenant and the need for something new. Ezekiel's prophecy is important in that he perceives more precisely the lack of the old desert covenant, which is the need of the *agency* of the Holy Spirit of God in this gracious operation on the heart in order for the covenant to be fulfilled. He says, "I will put my Spirit within you" בקרבכם ואת־רוחי אתן (Ezek 36:25–27).

Daniel

The prophet Daniel was "highly esteemed," or "precious," or "coveted" חמודות (Dan 9:23). We can, therefore, assume that we should pay attention to his writings with special confidence. Daniel provides a significant confession of both the great grace shown toward Israel and the sinful rebellion and failure of the people, according to the Torah narrative. This scroll is his basis for both the indictment of the failed experiment of the covenanted nation (the great majority according to the external call) and his understanding of the curse that has befallen her (Dan 9:11, 13). Not only does he charge Israel with rebellion against the Mosaic stipulations found in the Torah, but he also adds that she has disregarded the prophets who spoke in the name of Yahweh, "Moreover, we have not listened to your servants the prophets, who spoke in your name" אשר דברו בשמך ולא שמענו אל־עבדיך הנביאים (Dan 9:6). He clearly regards that the teachings of the Torah were set before the people through God's servants the prophets, who should certainly have been obeyed (Dan 9:10). Daniel stresses that to have disobeyed the prophets was the same as to disobey God himself (Dan 9:11).

It is very telling that Daniel has such a reverence for the scripture of the Torah as basically didactive in nature, that he learns from it how the curse (which is not a commandment *per se*) has come by God, confirming his word (Dan 9:12–13; see Deut 29:12). Along with his conviction of the inspiration of the Torah narrative, Daniel also holds the conviction that the prophecies of those raised up by the Spirit of God, such as the prophet Jeremiah, were also inspired and to be revered (Dan 9:2). This is perfectly consistent with what Isaiah had said earlier concerning the one who genuinely loves God—that the one who fears Yahweh also obeys his servant (Is 50:10). To listen to the prophets is to give attention to God's truth, which will always involve repentance from disobedience; as Daniel states, "by turning from our iniquity and giving attention to your truth" לשוב מעוננו ולהשכיל באמתך (Dan 9:13).

Daniel was favored with a significant revelation that speaks of the resolution to the tensions involved in the history of Israel. The failed and unrealized national covenant, and the problem of sin in the people who were supposed to love and glorify Yahweh, were problematic from the standpoint of God's will for a redeemed people to live for his glory and honor in the midst of a depraved and dark world.

The divine solution is declared briefly with terse expressions, some of which are not easy to decipher. But enough is provided that clearly indicates the power and wisdom of God to bring about *a victorious redress to the historical disappointments* that we have been studying, and this specifically through the mission of the coming Messiah. "Seventy weeks have been decreed for your people and your holy city" (Dan 9:24). The angel

Gabriel picks up the term alluding to seventy years of exile and essentially coins a new term as he duplicates it, in that he speaks the term for "weeks" as a masculine rather than a feminine term, as it normally would be: *shavuim* שבעים rather than *shavuot* שבעות. He probably expressed a poetic rather than rigid figure for a determined longer amount of time: "seventy sevens".

A number of years have been determined for the continuation of the old covenant stipulations and manner of relationship with God, until Messiah the Prince comes to the second temple that would be built. He comes to "finish the transgression, to make and end of sin, to make atonement for iniquity, to bring in everlasting righteousness" צדק עלמים לכלא הפשע ולהתם חטאת ולכפר עון ולהביא (Dan 9:24). That is, the need for the various animal sacrifices that were stipulated under Moses and which served as types will be fulfilled and done away with, and an everlasting righteousness and real spiritual atonement sacrifice will be provided to God's people through the coming of the Messiah. He will certainly come and accomplish this atonement before the destruction of the sanctuary and Jerusalem, which occurred in 70 CE. The Messiah will then be "cut off," or killed, after which another prince to come will "destroy the city and the sanctuary"—certainly, Titus of the Romans (Dan 9:26).

The work of the coming Messiah is, in fact, the goal of the revelations with which Daniel and the foregoing prophets were favored. These accomplishments were designed "to seal up vision and prophecy (prophet), and to anoint the most holy" ולחתם חזון ונביא ולמשח קדש קדשים (Dan 9:24). There will be no more need of the ministry of prophets, because it will have completed its purpose, which is to bring in the ministry of the Leading Anointed One (See Heb 1:1); nor of anointed rulers, because the Messiah Prince is the fulfillment of the typical Israelite kings and the consummate anointed ruler.

So then, according to the understanding of Daniel, the beloved prophet of God, we have these firm facts:

1. The Torah is didactive as well as prescriptive;

2. Yahweh should have been loved for his grace;

3. Israel is a failure according to the national covenant;

4. The prophets, along with the Torah, are to be obeyed as speaking God's truth;

5. A delimited time was divinely determined for the old covenant experiences;

6. The coming Messiah will have fulfilled and accomplished a perfect atonement and an everlasting righteousness, just before the destruction of the second temple.

Hosea

Significant *references and allusions* to the elements of the Torah narrative are found in the book of Hosea. It is clearly seen that the prophet regarded and utilized the Pentateuchal record as primarily a didactive document that speaks of the great grace of God toward the rescued people of Israel, and their arrogance, ingratitude, and sinful failure respecting the covenant to be his special people. Through Hosea's commission, God repudiates the spiritual relationship between Israel and himself, declaring that Israel is "not his people," and he is "not their God," because of their failure to keep the national covenant (Hos 1:9). This disproves the idea that Israel's relationship with God is guaranteed by her ethnic heritage. Indeed, because Israel disregarded the grace of God toward them, they are threatened with a return to Egypt (Hos 8:11–14).

True to the revelation of the Torah, however, as God chose the Patriarchs for covenant engagement and then the Hebrews over other ethnic groups to be his possession, so he demonstrates again his sovereignty in the matter of granting favor to a sinful people, determining that the Kingdom of Judah will be delivered by his compassion (Hos 1:6–7). Even though the "many instructions" רבי תורתי given to Israel are mentioned, the concern is not that they were not observed with precision, but that they were regarded as "strange things." Israel did not have the internal love for Yahweh that would have induced the care to keep the laws in sincerity and reverence (Hos 8:12).

Alluding to the significant statements in the song of indictment of Moses (Deut 32:10–25), Hosea recounts how God had graciously made the Israelites his people and improved their lives. They were to know no other god except him, but they had become proud when they were sated and forsook him. Therefore, God will be as a fierce beast that tears its prey to the people of Israel for their arrogance and ingratitude toward him (Hos 5:14—6:1; Hos 13:4–8). Israel was sated with Yahweh's provision yet proved to be a disappointment to him. But then God testifies to the greater importance of his having the constant internal love from his people rather than the mere external sacrifices of the covenant stipulations (Hos 6:6), thereby proving that (despite the continuance of external ritual) it is internal treachery that offends God (Hos 6:7).

The prophet clearly references the solemn pronouncement of God's fearful sovereignty also recorded in the song of indictment of Moses, stating, "It is I who put to death and give life. I have wounded, and it is I who heal," and that, "there is no one who can deliver from my hand," with nearly the same language ואין מידי מציל (Hos 5:14; Hos 6:1; see Deut 32:39). God refers to the Torah account of the patriarchs Judah and especially his father Jacob, the father of all Israel (Hos 12:2–5). Though Jacob started life being evil in taking his brother by the heel and pursuing a life of manipulation and dishonesty, in his maturity as a distressed man, he sought God's favor aggressively. In his earlier years, Jacob pursued a life of arrogant self-sufficiency, but then being humbled through difficulties—especially through an encounter with the living God—he learned his spiritual need for his Creator, begging with tears for divine favor rather than exhibiting haughty expectancy. "He wept and sought (implored) his favor" בכה ויתחנן לו (Hos 12:4). So then, the people of Israel should also repent of their arrogance and waywardness, and return to God, observe lovingkindness and justice, and wait continually for their God (Hos 12:6). Then the waiting will not be haughty expectation but spiritual appreciation of the grace of God.

The prophet perceives from the Torah account the important spiritual requirement that Israel be authoritatively led only by the prophets that God would commission for their redemptive lives, even as he had done so with Israel during their initial deliverance and guidance through the ministry of Moses (Hos 12:13). Hosea, therefore, should have been heeded. And today, Jesus the Messiah should be heeded for salvation (Matt 17:1–5; Heb 1:1–2).

Besides the Torah's assessment of the general failure of the nation of Israel (Deut 32:5–6), Hosea also expresses, in so many words, the core revelation of the Torah that God will nevertheless give his grace to Israel in "alluring her" and "betrothing" them to himself in the bond of a steadfast spiritual marriage. The people will be restored to him because of the influence of God's sovereign power in their lives, specifically through changing their hearts (Deut 30:6). This will come about not by their spiritual inability, which is only bent toward sin (being left to their own nature, as the Torah abundantly portrays), but because God will freely love them and powerfully heal their waywardness (Hos 2:14–23; Hos 14:4–8).

We see through the ministry of Hosea that God *recalls many passages* of the Torah, but none of it has to do with the anxiety of *halakha*. It is the internal love and glad reliance, shown in the heeding of his prophets' communications to his people, which God seeks.

Amos

The prophet Amos was ordinarily a shepherd and a grower of sycamore figs south of Jerusalem, but was suddenly commissioned by God to prophesy to the professionally religious and arrogant royal court at Bethel, in the northern kingdom of Israel (Amos 7:10–15). Though Amos was not an official prophet, God sovereignly chose to sharply rebuke rebellious and smug Israel through him. Most of his prophesying involves condemnation for Israel and Judah as well as various heathen nations, in such a manner that it shows up the *shameful equality of moral depravity* between them. That is, Israel is no better and no more pleasing to Yahweh than the pagans when she chooses to live disobedient to covenantal claims. This is evinced by the repeated formula of rebuke regarding either the heathen nations or Israel and Judah: "For three transgressions, and for four, etc." (Amos 1:3, 6, 11, 13 and Amos 2:1, 4, 6). Because of covenantal disobedience, Israel's deliverance from Egypt becomes no more significant than the movements of other nations within God's general providence, who enjoyed no favored relationship with him (Amos 9:7).

God has Amos reprove Israel for sinful infidelity to the Mosaic covenant. In doing so, God *recalls* certain important events and principles from the Torah, reaffirming that the Pentateuchal document is the *standard* by which sin and its judgment may be certainly known, and also God's sovereign terms of redemption and acceptance before his holiness. Yahweh reminds Israel how he set his redemptive attention on her alone and not on any other "families of the earth." But the whole family of Israel (the current generation as well as their fathers) was a disappointing *failure* in the national covenant-experiment and, therefore, despite the depravity of the other nations, was especially deserving of divine punishment (Amos 2:4; Amos 3:1–2; Amos 5:25–27).

Yahweh protested how he judged Israel harshly just as he had done *during the earlier Pentateuchal era* (Amos 4:10–11). Though the official religionists practiced a form of Mosaic worship, its emptiness was despised by God (Amos 5:21–23). What can be seen in the pre-exilic book of Amos, as well as many other books and psalms of the Hebrew Bible, is that the Torah narrative and the later history of the monarchic period seem to be well known because they are *referenced as common knowledge* (Amos 4:10–11; Amos 5:25; Amos 6:5; Amos 9:11). Again, what is recalled and discussed are the historical interactions between God and his people within their redemptive relationship, and not the anxiety of *halakha.*

Amos emphasizes that the office of prophet was the divine means of *communicating the mind* and will of God, and therefore the prophets should have been heeded (Amos 3:7; Amos 4:13; see Deut 18:15–18). So then, through this prophet—who was surprisingly commissioned as a current spokesman—God warns of the judgment of a "famine of hearing the words of the Lord" (Amos 8:11–12). They will be made to feel the misery of not having authentic communication, direction, or comfort from God in their time of distress. This has especially proven true during the intertestamental period, lasting 400 years.

It is important to notice that the true spiritual glory of David's kingdom was regarded as a *fallen booth.* But Amos provides some predictive words of glorious restoration for the kingdom of Israel, and the sway of the renewed Davidic reign will be extensive, prosperous, and secure. Israel will never be uprooted again from the land God gave to them (Amos 9:11–15).

Micah

The prophet Micah, the contemporary of the prophet Isaiah, who also predicted the Babylonian captivity because of Israel's sinfulness, was probably a peasant farmer from the countryside of Jerusalem, and probably with no significant pedigree. Yet it was this humble man that God used to speak of the weightier matters of his revelation to the covenanted people of Israel. Consistent with other biblical writers, the prophet regards, not the pristine performance of the bare letter of the Law but the general spiritual failure of Israel and Judah to keep the spirit of the covenant with which they were so amazingly graced by the kindness of

God toward their fathers. He denounces the shameful disobedience and spiritual falsehood of the privileged rulers, prophets, and priests, who performed their roles and offices for selfish gain while they relied on the outward trappings of organized religion—such as the presence of the material temple, and claiming from this that Yahweh is in their midst (Mic 3:1–12; see Isa 48:1–2; Jer 7:4).

Micah also preaches the amazing disclosure of *the divinely appointed and righteous coming ruler* that will reign over a truly devoted Israel and will establish the age of righteousness and peace (Mic 5:2–5). This ruler from the tribe of Judah will be especially provided by the sovereign determination and unshakable purpose of Yahweh, who in turn will serve him ("for me" לי) with his whole soul (Mic 5:2), whose origins, God says, were "from of old, from the days of a previous era" (Author's translation.) ומוצאתיו מקדם מימי עולם (See also Mic 7:14–15, 20). That is, this prediction is *intimated and rooted in the Torah* concerning the permanent royal characterization of the tribe of Judah (Gen 49:10; see Mic 7:14). This promised coming ruler will, in fact, be God in the person of a son of man, the child born of a woman, for "he will arise and shepherd his flock in the strength of the Lord (Yahweh) and in the majesty of the name of the Lord his God" ועמד ורעה בעז יהוה בגאון שם יהוה אלהיו (Mic 5:3–4).

Yahweh, in the setting of a lawsuit, complains emphatically that he has shown great grace and kindness to Israel, but that they have not spiritually appreciated this favor and loved him in return. Again, the Torah narratives are appealed to for the facts of Israel's redemption from the slavery of Egypt and the provision of godly leadership in Moses, Aaron, and Miriam. Israel was greatly blessed but they failed to be grateful and holy. But God was righteous in all his ways with them (Mic 6:1–5). It is important to understand that these divine interactions are the weightier concerns of the scroll of the Torah for the prophet and not the supposed anxiety over the precise performance of the *mitzvot*. The commandments were indeed expected to be observed, but with the reasonableness and latitude that comes with the core attitude of sincere love for God that even an unsophisticated, peasant, godly, farmer such as Micah of Moresheth can be found to have.

This point is sustained by the very telling verses that follow the general indictment by God. Micah plainly minimizes the role of the prescribed sacrifices commanded in the Torah and even imagines hyperbolically the sacrificing of his own children as useless, because they are nothing and can do nothing when it concerns the attitude of the heart toward God (Mic 6:6–7; see Isa 29:13). Nothing else can make up for this duty. If a man does not love God and accordingly does not serve him with the whole heart's affection, then none of his outward offerings, no matter how costly or magnificent, can please God in the way only real love for him can. These vain offerings are then proven to be born from pride, self-satisfaction, or an attempt to appease the mere conscience. Such worldly attitudes can never produce real love for God. Micah appropriately declares Israel's humiliated position as mere men before the Creator, and asseverates what God has plainly required from his people—that they should live with sound judgment, to love kindness, and to behave humbly in the sight of God (Mic 6:8).

The requirements of the Torah are neatly summarized as demanding true love and humility toward God, which will in turn ensure the correct observation of the stipulations of the covenant. But it is essential to understand that the most important requirement of the Torah was *the soul governed by the divine honor* and not the performance of ritual. *Rabbinic halakha* cannot be justified. Finally, it is again the significant *divine interactions and revelations recorded in the Torah* that are foundational and controlling for the faith and hope of Micah and all those who are God's possession (Mic 7:18–20). These things occupy the prophet's mind and not the details of *halakha*.

Malachi

Probably the last of the writing prophets, Malachi addresses the spiritual conditions of the Jewish returnees from Babylonian captivity—there was much sin, disobedience, and covenantal failure, just as there had been before the punishment of exile. The divine punishment of exile *did not really change* what needed to be changed in order for the people to be the loving and obedient servants that God demanded. There were such things as insincere and unacceptable offerings by the priests (Mal 1:6–14), the priests were not reverencing God's covenant with Levi (Mal 2:1–9), and there was idolatry and divorce (Mal 2:10–16). It is clear from this book that the great and glorious advantages of the unmerited favor, kindness, and just laws of God toward the descendants of Jacob (as is found within the Torah), and the divine wrath expressed for disobedience, did not produce the true spiritual and righteous relationship that God commanded.

And the very reason that these advantages did not produce the desired result is because of what the earlier prophets had already revealed.

Beginning with Moses and culminating in Jeremiah and Ezekiel, they revealed the need for the Spirit of God to supernaturally change the hearts of those whom Yahweh would have as his own devoted servants in truth and righteousness. But Malachi discloses the obvious fact that among the general populace, *such a divine transformation had not yet taken place* despite the humbling catastrophe of the destruction of the temple and the Babylonian exile. The great and glorious descriptions of future universal Jewish spiritual devotion in the land, discussed below, have not yet been realized. There was yet to be fulfilled the promises of a new and better covenantal relationship, which we saw Jeremiah and Ezekiel had predicted.

In Malachi, we see some significant evidences that the New Covenant had not yet been inaugurated. One is that "the messenger of the covenant" was yet to come to his temple; that is, Yahweh himself will come to his temple in a sudden and unexpected manner, "and the Lord, whom you seek, will suddenly come to his temple" אֲשֶׁר־אַתֶּם מְבַקְשִׁים וּפִתְאֹם יָבוֹא אֶל־הֵיכָלוֹ הָאָדוֹן —to the second temple before it would be destroyed. It is to "his temple" אֶל־הֵיכָלוֹ that this messenger comes. Only Yahweh can call the temple his temple. This is undoubtedly the same Servant of Yahweh predicted by Isaiah because he is appointed as "a covenant to the people" (See Isa 42:1–9; Isa 49:8). It is Yahweh himself who will come as a messenger, because no one will be able to endure the fiery purification of his appearance. Only Yahweh can refine the sons of Levi so that "they might present offerings in righteousness" (Mal 3:1–4).

There is also a more pronounced principle introduced that encourages a more conscious distinguishing between those who truly feared God and esteemed his name and those who did not. There is to be a sharp and clear discernment "between the righteous and the wicked, between one who serves God and one who does not serve him" (Mal 3:16, 18). So then, not everyone who was involved in this national covenant upon the return from exile (and many did not return who were in love with their newfound secular advantages) was any more changed and committed than those Israelites of previous generations who were confronted by the rebuking prophets.

It is also clear that those who had returned from exile were to live and observe the original Mosaic national covenant with its statutes and ordinances, as God commanded, "Remember the law of Moses my ser-vant" זכרו תורת משה עבדי; which no doubt included the original temple service and priesthood inaugurated through Moses, and which had not as yet been displaced by the inauguration of the New Covenant (Mal 4:4). This alone refutes the rabbinic ideas of a supposed continued covenantal relationship with God without a temple, priesthood, or blood sacrifice. God never says that the Mosaic cultic regulations may be substituted with prayer and good works. God himself never abrogates these things, and so the rabbis taught falsehood and disobedience.

The New Testament

Finally, in the Jewish writings of the Greek New Testament, the *recollec-tions of the Torah* are not merely the aspect of the Law, though it is often referred to in honor of its character of the divine standard for holiness and morality. Often, it is the profound initial events of the Pentateuchal narrative concerning the interactions of God with his called people in the fathers and the nation of Israel, revealing the character and the sover-eignty of his grace, how that nation failed historically, and the correlative disclosures of grace that is necessary and also promised in fulfillment of the redemptive purposes of God toward mankind. The important texts are the judgments of the Messiah Jesus found in the gospels (Matt 23:29–35; John 8:37, 44, 47); Stephen's defense in the book of Acts (Acts 7:17–43, 51–53); the relevant passages in the book of Hebrews (Heb 3:7–12, 16–19; Heb 4:2; Heb 8:7–9); and the declaration of Peter concerning the function of the prophets of old, how they prophesied of the grace of salvation to come (1 Pet 1:10–12).

Therefore, without doubt, *the safest and most accurate understanding* of the purpose of the Torah is gathered by considering the usage of this re-vered scroll by the prophets, in what they perceive and what they say in light of this corpus of revelation. Indeed, this same principle is the basis for refuting all abuses of the Holy Scriptures. Whether it is the anti-Mo-saic, mythical, and mystical extremes of rabbinic Judaism, or some of the groundless extremes of Christianity, they will all be exposed as erroneous when honestly examined in the light of the understanding of the Hebrew prophets.

Torah of Sin and Grace

For evangelical Christianity, the ultimate understanding of the Torah is also found *reflected in the minds of Jesus and Paul.* The prophetic
development of the rest of the Tanakh, and eventually the inspired ad-
denda of the Greek New Testament proclaiming the Tanakh's fulfillment,
can be viewed as essentially the inspired interpretation of, or the inspired
development of, the message and purpose of the great principal scroll of
the Torah. These provide much commentary upon the understanding of
this revered document, as well as the disclosure of the intentions of God
through it.

So then, not only were the moral, ceremonial, and civil commandments to be taught, but also the divine displeasure and judgments in
response to sin and rebellion were to be a very real part of Israel's instruction, as indeed it was recorded. There are, in fact, ominous curses that
were to be taught to the people as well as the promises of blessing for
loyalty to Yahweh (Deut 27:11–26; Deut 28:1–68). And the indictment of
Israel spoken by Moses, which we will see, is very telling as to the general
didactic nature of the Torah; for he sings, "Let my discourse לקחי drop
as the rain, my speech distill as the dew," and then proceeds to discuss the
recent narrative of Israel's covenant infidelity (Deut 32:2).

When the above passages are carefully considered regarding the
question of the purpose of the Torah in the minds of the godly ones of
ancient Israel, we see that it was rather different from what rabbinic Judaism imagines it to be. It is not the fodder of punctilious and fastidious
refinement of keeping the letter of the laws found within the Torah. It
is not the matrix of dead and dry material for formulating perfunctory
religion and ritual. It is not a text from which to launch the tedious and
imaginative wanderings and meanderings of rabbinic *midrashim*. In reality and practice, the Jews exalt and revere the sayings of the sages found
in the Talmud and other traditions above the teachings of Moses and the
prophets. These rabbinic practices were not of the piety of the prophets
and those few genuine fellow *chasidim* among their generations. These
rabbinic abuses are the natural result of the invented religion that sup-
plants the Mosaic traditions, demonstrated pointedly by the fact that they
deem, without divine authority, half of the covenant stipulations unnec-
essary, along with no temple sacrifice or priesthood.

Rabbinic Judaism in all its orthodox or secular forms is intellectually
dishonest in that it flatters itself as "keeping Torah," as Paul observes (Rom
2:17–20), when half of the Torah is dismissed without divine authority in

reaction to the providential destruction of the temple and Israel's dispersion (which were because of their rejection of the messages of the later prophets concerning the Messiah Jesus, the better sacrifice, and the better priesthood). And even though rabbinic Jews hold the attitude that they are pleasing to God in their exacting traditions, they cannot satisfactorily explain why God has not forgiven and restored them to their former national glory. If they were judged, as the rabbis confessed early on, "for our sins," then why has God not restored them, since they feel they do well in "keeping Torah" for the past two thousand years?

But in practice, as they hold the narrow and debilitating regard of the Torah as mainly a corpus of laws for their culture, rabbinic Jews pursue this denatured document as the metric to which they strive to approximate personal conformity to a purely human, external, earthly behavior—a conformity that ultimately thrives on personal, fleshly pride of works-righteousness. Their most basic reliance of acceptance with God is the merit of their presumed near conformity to the letter of the laws as they read them. This is, in reality, a salvation by personal works-righteousness that contravenes the grace of God granting an unmerited justification of life. But as we will see, the account of Abraham being justified through faith in God militates against this rabbinic notion of acceptance with God.

Rather, as asserted earlier, the godly writers of the Bible see the purpose of the Torah as not only the record of the stipulations of the covenant but an embodiment of profound initial manifestations having primarily a didactive character, to which *all theologizing must refer for validation.* It is revered as the norm and controlling doctrinal standard, not only of the moral will of God concerning the divine covenant, but also of the fearful principle of sin and the sovereign character of God's grace in redemption. More particularly, they regard it as the principal record of the divine interventions and interactions, which reveals the nature of man's sin and the nature of God's grace in response to his condition. The Torah is seen as the unveiling of the beginnings of God's redemptive purposes for all mankind through the election of the Hebrews. The Law assumes a history.

5

The Profound Teachings of the Torah

EMBEDDED WITHIN THE PENTATEUCHAL narrative are many profound declarations, or verses that contain *momentous disclosures*. They are profound because these disclosures are patently relevant to the concerns between any man and God; that is, they have ramifications *for all of humanity* and are not, in their nature, delimited to Israel. These are revelations that are *not mere narrative* of historical Israel. They directly teach us the fear that is due God and how to feel our need for him, or they directly teach the glory of his goodness for those who love him. But the profound disclosures that are specifically intended for Israel are declarations that transcend the stipulations of the Mosaic covenant, such as the sovereign decrees of Israel's destiny. The prophets who saw their priority in revelation sometimes reiterate them in later scripture, or their substance is employed in their speeches, or they form the background for new revelations.

Only some of these scattered disclosures are here discussed that are directly relevant to the argument of this book. Many of these declarations are very much an important part of the divine instructions conveyed as special revelation given to Israel; therefore, *they are not to be minimized and overlooked* as though only the laws *per se* are important for God's people to heed. All of the words of condemnation, and all of the declarations of God's character, and all of the divine comments, and all of the disclosures of God's sovereign purposes are to be reverently regarded along with the words of grace that God will provide, even as much as the prescription of law for his worship.

Indeed, these profound declarations are inherently more important than the legal codes because they disclose the mind of God on such a high level that to miss them and dim one's sight in focusing only on the laws leads to a deceptive misapprehension of God's purpose for the laws. And when the laws are isolated from the larger context of divine relation, there inevitably arises the false notion that the keeping of the law is the expected way of meriting a right standing with God.

The laws are covenant obligations for walking in fellowship with God but which also contain regulations for the events of sin that *ipso facto* prove the law cannot and did not intend to make a man perfectly righteous before God. The laws were not intended to provide the means to merit the justification of one's person before God, but to maintain *the prescribed conditions of loving responsiveness* for continued fellowship with him; which fellowship is begun by entering into the covenant established by God's grace designed to have and love a people through their faith in and loyalty to him. This covenant was given in kindness to the Hebrews while regarding the true state of their sinfulness and demerit; all of which conditions are found within the wider context of the Torah.

So then, these important disclosures are the results of God's holy interaction with his people, and *their knowledge is critical* in appreciating the narrative document of his initial saving activities; concerning which, it is an offence to God to regard lightly (See Isa 66:2). Only the most relevant declarations for this book's argument are here listed, followed by some key passages in the New Testament proving that Jesus and the Apostles taught only what the Tanakh taught:

The Sinfulness of Mankind

The universality of sin and the total depravity of the heart of man are unequivocally asserted as the present conditions of mankind due to his original defection from God (Gen 3:1–24). The definition of sin is clearly depicted here as the evil of both original disobedience and the consequent persistent disobedience to God's revealed will for man, which results in man's alienation from his Creator. The sacred writer asserts absolutely the tragic fact of mankind's profound corruption: "Then the Lord saw that the wickedness of man was great on the earth and that every intent of the thoughts of his heart was only evil continually" (Gen 6:5). The language of the text is *comprehensive and leaves no room for any natural goodness* in the heart of man. The mental devising of mankind's thoughts is "only evil all the day" רק רע כל־היום.

This does not mean that a man continually thinks of only morally perverse things, but rather that everything he thinks and does is ultimately *motivated not by the love and honor of God* but for the man's interests alone—and these things may or may not be evil toward another man. And again, "Now the earth was corrupt in the sight of God, and the earth was filled with violence. And God looked on the earth, and behold, it was corrupt; for all flesh had corrupted their way upon the earth." (Gen 6:11–12). These verses early on in the sacred scroll refute the rabbinic notion of the "impulse toward good" יצר־הטוב, which is supposedly found alongside the "impulse toward evil" יצר־הרע within man's inner nature.

The text and the prophets will not support the idea that man can freely choose the good over the evil in any real approved manner before the holy God. There is "only evil" רק רע, although there is relative "goodness" that is to be seen everywhere. The prophets consistently declare the fact of the depravity of mankind without any room for true goodness or natural ability for true goodness before God (1 Kgs 8:46; Ps 14:1–3; Ps 130:3; Ps 143:2; Jer 17:9). Personal moral deviation from the will of God is the first problem and first concern for man; therefore, sincere repentance of sin is essential for any change toward salvation from its guilt and judgment (Isa 55:6–7). This teaching is maintained in the NT (Matt 15:18–19; Mark 7:20–23; John 8:34–47; Rom 3:9–20; Rom 7:7–13; Rom 8:5–8; Eph 2:3; Titus 3:3).

The Afterlife

This great scroll of sacred literature early on indicates the reality of an afterlife, which has always been the unspoken wish or yearning of all people, but especially of those who have been made alive to God through grace. It is these especially who take seriously the inevitable and irrevocable state of everlasting existence—either with God or without God—according to his standing before the holy Creator. Enoch experienced an exceptional closeness with God, as he "walked with God" (Gen 5:22). The precious fact is repeated again (Gen 5:24). In both verses, it is stated with the *hithpael* form of הלך, meaning that he intentionally made himself walk with God; that is, *he desired to be close to God* in fellowship with him ויתהלך חנוך את־האלהים.

Through God's goodness and grace, he will have someone in loving fellowship with him because this was the original intention for mankind. The pleasure that God takes with those who are close to him in loving fellowship is indicated by the special favor God showed Enoch in "taking him" ואיננו כי־לקח אתו אלהים (Gen 5:24). There is no escaping the implications of this passage; there is an afterlife beyond this present life, though it is rarely adumbrated during the earlier biblical period. Enoch did not die as the others in the genealogy listed here, because "God took Him." If the present life is all there is to be experienced and annihilation is expected, then this event with Enoch was no sign of favor but of condemnation, for the Hebrews normally dreaded a premature cessation of their lives (See, for examples, Ps 102:24 and Isa 38:10).

Very often, the punitive judgment of being killed, or "cut off," by God is to be seen in the sacred narratives. But it is clear that Enoch was loved in a special manner by God and was rewarded with the favor of going to be with him directly without the experience of death. Even if we interpreted these expressions as metaphorical of death, still it must be seen as a reward for Enoch's close piety. Annihilation is not a just reward for piety toward the living God, but rather an affront to God's character—he would appear ridiculous dispensing the same final reward to both the pious and the rebellious! What honor is due to God? What encouragement to us?

There is occasional testimony by the prophets to the fact of an afterlife. The taking up of Elijah *directly to heaven* is consistent with the account of Enoch and corroborates the reality of perpetual existence for man (2 Kgs 2:11–12). In Isaiah, the predictions of the great and glorious restoration of the nation of Israel are stated in terms of the everlasting and unshakable duration of the salvific blessedness of the redeemed compared to even the determined change of the heavens and earth, and the sure destruction of the haters of the godly ones (Isa 51:6–8). Along with the more intimate spiritual worship that is to be seen in the expressions of the psalmists and later prophets is the cherished conviction and hope of being found in the heavenly presence of God as the godly man's ultimate reward for his devotion—and conversely, a miserable afterlife for the wicked (Ps 16:10–11; Ps 17:14–15; Ps 49:14–15; Ps 73:4, 19, 23–26; Isa 26:19; Isa 66:24; Dan 12:2).

Concerning the afterlife of damnation for the wicked, it is this author's opinion that God adumbrates the punishment of everlasting misery in the utterance of fierce wrath found in the song of indictment spoken by

Moses (Deut 32:22). God vehemently declares that "a fire is kindled in my anger, and burns to the lowest part of Sheol." That it goes on to "consume the earth and its yield, and sets on fire the foundations of the mountains" seems to be a strained effort to express an extraordinary anger that destroys existence as it was known to man.

The destruction of geological aspects of life is hardly the real intent of this wrath, but must mean something terrifying to those who are destroyed in punitive judgment. It becomes rather clear later in the prophets that not only is there a resurrection of the condemned for everlasting "disgrace" and "abhorrence" (Dan 12:2), but that they will be subject to everlasting misery *denoted by fire*, of which they will be conscious because their "worm will not die" (Isa 66:24). This teaching is maintained in the NT (Matt 25:31–46; Mark 9:38–48; John 5:25–29; John 11:21–26; Acts 23:6–8; Rom 8:11; 1 Cor 15:1–57; Phil 3:20–21; Col 3:1–4; 1 Thess 4:13–18; Heb 12:22–24; Rev 20:11–15).

Redemption Through a Man

After the first humans, Adam and Eve, are exposed as rebellious and the deceiving "serpent" is cursed, God mercifully asserts a brief notice of *hope* for the humans. The well-known tension between people and snakes is employed to depict the subsequent spiritual struggle between God and Satan that will be experienced in the realm of mankind. The promise of hope here is that though humanity's relationship with God has been ruined, God will gain the victory and *repair* it through the *surprising agency of a member* of that ruined race. A particular male offspring will destroy the "serpent" (and consequently, his bad effects), but he will also experience some harm from him (Gen 3:14–15).

This verse is not specifically a messianic prediction, but it is important to understand that this discloses the sovereign determination to restore the original divine intention for human fellowship through the *mediation of a human being*. It is also important to realize that the writer(s) of the Torah did not compose its narratives vainly, but had theological intentions in conveying divine truths. The account of the "offspring" of the woman uses the same term for the "offspring" of Abraham זרע, when God declared great and glorious redemptive promises within the realization of the Covenant of Grace (Gen 22:18). All the nations of the earth would eventually be blessed *through Abraham's offspring.* Within Abraham's calling, we see the focused beginning of God's resolve to fulfill his redemptive purposes of repairing the breach induced by the serpent's deceit. This divine resolve becomes even more particular within *the Davidic dynasty's offspring,* where a "child will be born" for Judah—both for a sign of national comfort for King Uzziah and, still later, for spiritual redemption and rule through the appearing of the *son given who will be known as Yahweh himself* (Isa 7:14; Isa 9:6–7). This teaching is maintained in the NT (Matt 4:13–16; Acts 3:25–26; Rom 16:20; Gal 3:16; Rev 12:5).

The Grace of Salvation

The call of Abraham and the giving of the covenant—for him to have El Shaddai as his God and for Abraham and his seed to be Elohim's people—are sheer grace and glorious determination (Gen 12:1–3; Gen 17:1–8). The glorious sunshine of God's determined pronouncements to redeem a people—to save a people from the judgment for sin through the granting of unmerited grace and to grant a loving and intimate relationship with himself—is *first given to the Hebrews* (Exod 3:18) but is intended to include all peoples. The *eventual inclusion of the gentiles* is within the purview of God's redemptive purposes through the Covenant of Grace established with Abraham ונברכו בך כל משפחת האדמה (Gen 12:3; Gen 18:18; Gen 22:18; Gen 26:4; Gen 28:14; Ps 67:1–7; Isa 42:6; Isa 49:6). This initial grace—the covenant with Abraham—*opens the door* and provides the way and means for man to be reconciled to God.

Real salvation from sinful alienation from God always springs from his pure unmerited grace. It was by sheer grace that God called Abram from Sumerian idol–worship and determined to set his love upon him and Isaac and Jacob (Deut 4:37; Deut 7:7–8; Josh 24:2–3). Abram was not found by God to be a "good man" among idolaters but was actually redeemed from a life of spiritual darkness (Josh 24:2–3; Isa 29:22). It was because of unwavering determined love toward these fathers, according to his promised covenant of grace with them, that Yahweh resolved to establish a redemptive relationship with the children of Israel; it was not induced by any considered necessity or greatness of them (Deut 7:6–8). Also, when the children of Israel had actually been given the Promised

Land, it was not due to any righteousness of their own, for that characterization is denied them (Deut 9:4–6).

The prophets consistently affirm that the basis of the committed faithfulness of God toward the children of Israel is to be found in the original covenant with Abraham, Isaac, and Jacob (Ps 105:37–45; Mic 7:20). More than this, the prophets preach the fact of God's promised resolve to bless "all the families of the earth," with the same loving relationship as the Hebrews were to enjoy, will be realized with the eventual inclusion of the gentiles within that very covenant with Abraham (Ps 67:1–7; Isa 19:18–24; Isa 42:6; Isa 49:6; Isa 51:4; Isa 52:10).

The gentiles who are redeemed should feel profound gratitude to God for his kindness in *extending* his sovereign grace to them through the blessedness of the salvation first granted to the Hebrews, and they should extend *honor* to the Jewish people wherever they are encountered. Israel is the cultivated olive tree planted by Yahweh, but the wild branches of the gentiles *were grafted onto this tree*. The gentiles are therefore *utterly dependent* upon the means of salvation that was first provided to the Jews (Rom 11:11–24). The Jews are to be *loved as Hebrew persons* because they were first given God's love and calling.

The prophets also consistently recognize that the real essence of the blessedness of the Abrahamic covenant is the enjoyment of a personal, loving, and intimate relationship with God (Jer 24:7; Jer 30:22; Jer 31:33; Jer 32:38; Ezek 36:28). This teaching is maintained in the NT (John 3:14–18; John 5:24; John 6:33, 40; John 10:9–10, 28; Acts 3:25–26; Rom 1:16–17; Rom 3:23–26; 2 Cor 5:17–21; 2 Cor 6:16–18; Gal 4:4–7; Eph 2:4–10; 2 Thess 2:13–14; Titus 3:4–7; 1 Pet 2:9–10; 2 Pet 1:2–4; 1 John 1:5–7).

The Necessary Condition of Faith

The Torah reveals that it is necessary that a person's right standing before God be obtained only through sincere belief in the revelation given by God. We find the important text stating that *through believing with loving reliance* (or trusting) in God's revelation, Abraham was *accounted as righteous and acceptable* before God והאמן ביהוה ויחשבה לו צדקה (Gen 15:6). This enunciates the important principle that, within the forgoing context of the universal and total depravity of mankind, there is no possibility of a man being able to be found truly and thoroughly righteous before God, but that he must be accounted חשב righteous צדקה before him only by his gracious regard. Only then will a man be truly acceptable to God and admitted into his spiritual presence, and loved as his child.

Along with this necessary faith, or loving reliance, is the necessary condition of wholehearted repentance from any and all known sin or immorality. Abram was called to leave his lifestyle of Babylonian idolatry, and the rescued Hebrew slaves were to live in a new and highly ethical manner than the cultural environs of Egypt or Canaan. Repentance is unmistakably demanded by God (Lev 26:40; Ps 7:12; Ps 32:5; Isa 55:6–7; Ezek 20:43; Ezek 36:31; Hos 14:1–3). Moreover, this text, describing Abraham's trust in God's disclosures, refutes the notion that a man could be justified before God by any personal goodness due to law-keeping. Otherwise, the sacred author would have stated such an eventuation somewhere in the sacred text, especially for Abraham.

Undoubtedly, Abraham lived in the fear of God (known then as El Shaddai) after his calling into covenantal fellowship with him, in that according to the general tenor of his conduct, he obeyed the moral requirements of his conscience and the established laws of the lands where he sojourned, since the Sinai code had not yet been given to his descendants. Nevertheless, the text is clear and the concept is unassailable; that because of Abraham's trust in God's words, which involved Abraham cleaving to God's character, God regarded him righteous and acceptable. And if this right standing was accorded because of his belief, then the implication is that there was *no room left* for the merit of personal righteousness.

God has once for all revealed in this passage of the Torah how he intends to regard a man righteous before him: it is to be by faith in God's offered grace. Again, this regard is gracious because it is not due to any supposed perfect fulfillment of ethical demands; rather, it is a free and unmerited crediting of right standing. This text demonstrates that such a gracious regard of right standing comes only upon *the principle of believing Yahweh's revelations,* even as Abraham believed God והאמן ביהוה.

Again, the scriptures never state that Abraham was regarded righteous due specifically to his keeping the commandments of God; and, though he was exhorted to be sincere and faithful before God (Gen 17:1) we certainly know of his imperfect trust and his moral faults in the larger narrative. Consistent with Abraham's calling, the Mosaic covenant required that the children of Israel respond, in turn, to their calling to be a special people for Yahweh with loving faith (Exod 4:5, 31; Exod 14:31; Exod 19:9; Num 14:11; Num 20:12; Deut 1:32; Deut 9:23). The law was not intended to be a means of meriting justification before God but rather a means of prescribing the holiness that God required for his fellowship and honor. It was *the manner of loving response* in covenant fellowship and not the earning of divine justification.

By believing God's disclosures of himself and his will, the Israelites would have been accounted righteous and accepted before him, in their acceptance of the covenant relationship. With the conscious enjoyment of this new divine acceptance and relationship, they would only then have to express their love and gratitude in the peculiar manner of the Mosaic covenant stipulation. The prophets affirm this principle that faith in God's revelation is the condition of obtaining forgiveness of sin and a right standing with him, and is stated in various aspects (Ps 32:2; Ps 130:3–6; Ps 143:2; Isa 50:10; Isa 53:1; Isa 61:10; Jer 17:7–8; Jer 23:6; Hab 2:4). This teaching is maintained in the NT (Matt 4:17; Matt 13:16; John 1:12; John 3:16, 18; John 10:25–30; John 14:1; John 20:29–31; Rom 3:21–26; Rom 4:1–8; Rom 5:1; Rom 10:1–13; Gal 3:26–29; Eph 2:4–10; Phil 1:29; 1 Thess 2:13; 2 Thess 2:13–15; Jas 2:14–26; 2 Pet 1:1; Jude 20–21).

The Divine Election

In the account of the twins, Jacob and Esau, born to Isaac and Rebekah, we see an indisputable example of the divine election of one person over another for favor—even as the previous elections of the general lineages of Seth, Noah, and Abraham. God clearly determined the destinies of both twins even before their actual birth, which *ipso facto* precludes the regard of their moral character having a bearing beforehand, which is expressly denied. God decided before their births that the older will serve the younger, and that the blessing of the covenant of grace will be promoted through Jacob's lineage (Gen 25:23).

The divine election is sovereign in that there is nothing within the person regarded as motivating God's decision, and also that there is nothing outside of God's own secret council compelling him to decide a certain way. Neither the justice of God nor the needs of the creature require that God should elect anyone. It is determined by God's pleasure and will alone. The sovereignty of the election of Jacob over Esau is proven also in the inclusion of the destinies of the two resultant nations deriving from them, which would mean the disregard of many persons' moral character involved in the decreed plans for these nations.

We see also that not every Hebrew necessarily will be elected to be blessed with a loving relationship with God. Even though Ishmael was a son of Abraham, he was driven away with his mother Hagar and not included in the lineage that had the covenant promise of God (Gen 17:18–21). And Esau was a son of Isaac, but he was rejected and his descendants were cursed, because God had set his love upon Jacob and not Esau (Mal 1:2–4). And the great majority of the wilderness generation after the exodus were under the wrath of God and were ultimately rejected (Ps 95:8–11).

Consequently, it is usually a "remnant" of Israel that God wills to redeem or keep for himself, rather than all of Israel (1 Kgs 19:18; Isa 1:9; Isa 6:8–13; Isa 10:20–23; Isa 11:11–16; Isa 46:3–4; Joel 2:32; Amos 5:15). God elected to preserve Judah while not preserving the northern nation of Israel (Hos 1:6–7; Zech 1:17; Zech 2:12). In the global arena, God elected the Hebrew people to enjoy his salvific light while leaving the pagan nations in their darkness (Deut 7:6; Isa 60:1–2). Divine election is consistently revealed and taught in the Torah and the prophets (Deut 4:34, 37; Deut 33:4–5; Ps 4:3; Ps 7:6–7; Ps 65:4; Ps 105:6; Ps 135:4; Isa 6:8–13; Mal 1:2–3). This teaching is maintained in the NT (Matt 11:25–26; John 6:37; John 15:16, 19; John 17:2, 6, 9, 24; Acts 13:48; Acts16:14; Rom 9:10–18; Rom 11:1–7; 1 Cor 1:26–31; Eph 1:4–11; Phil 1:6, 29; 1 Thess 1:4–5; 1 Thess 5:9; 2 Tim 1:9; Jas 1:18; 1 Pet 1:1–2; 1 Pet 2:9–10; 2 Pet 1:1).

The Sovereignty of Grace

After the golden calf incident, when Moses intercedes to effect atonement between God and the people who had sinned, Moses pleads that Yahweh would resume his presence and leading of the Israelites as his covenant people—and Moses succeeds in imploring God to show him his glory in a special manner. Yahweh concedes to Moses' requests and decides to show him his goodness, which would involve forgiveness and reconciling himself to the Israelites again. But Yahweh quickly adds, concerning this matter of his goodness toward sinners, that he will be "gracious to whom he decides to be gracious," and he will be "compassionate to whom he decides to be compassionate" אֶת־אֲשֶׁר אָחֹן וְרִחַמְתִּי אֶת־אֲשֶׁר אֲרַחֵם וְחַנֹּתִי (Exod 33:19). It will be God's sovereign decision alone and it will not be presumed upon, nor will it be given to everyone who, in fact, needs it. If the language in this verse (אֶת־אֲשֶׁר) does not emphasize that *it will depend only upon God's decision* and not be determined by the needs of every sinner, then the assertion means nothing.

The "grace" חֵן that is spoken of within the Torah is eventually seen to be rich with meaning and pregnant with various forms of manifestation that were not immediately understood nor thoroughly revealed during the earliest biblical period. It would take, according to the progressive revelation that was actually conducted by the Holy Spirit, later developments and later utterances of especially the latter prophets, and then fully manifested and explained with the coming of the Messiah Jesus. But the grace of God in the Torah concerning the Israelite cult specifically means the *unmerited decision to show mercy* by providing salvation for a sinful people (or to individuals among that people) through atonement and preservation; the provision of a means of forgiveness and atonement in the priesthood and animal sacrifice, a covenanted relationship, the giving of the law for holiness, and scripture for guidance and comfort.

But in the mind of God, there was a *greater grace* that was to be revealed later, in the enactment of a *better covenant* through the giving of the Holy Spirit who will provide *supernatural ability* to love God, to practice the laws, and to keep the covenant. And there will be given the fulfillment of the righteous demands of the law and the satisfaction of the penalty of guilt, typified in the animal sacrifices, in the person of the Messiah Jesus. This will be discussed more fully later. The prophets perceive and preach this fearful fact of the sovereignty of God's grace initially found in the divine revelation of the Torah (1 Sam 16:1–12; 2 Sam 7:8–17; Ps 65:4; Ps 78:67–71; Isa 1:9; Isa 6:8–13; Isa 10:20–23; Isa 11:11–16; Isa 46:3–4; Zeph 2:7; Zeph 3:12–13; Mal 1:1–5). This teaching is maintained in the NT (Mark 4:10–12; John 12:37–41; Rom 9:6–29; Rom 11:1–10; 1 Thess 5:9; 1 Pet 2:8).

The Glory of God's Love

When Yahweh wills to be gracious and compassionate to someone, he shows himself to be glorious in nature, being a very loving, compassionate, patient, and truthful God (Exod 34:6). This is God's essential goodness and loveliness, which will be seen and experienced by those who are brought into a close relationship with him. All of man's created and sal- vific needs are fully met in these attributes (Exod 20:6; Num 14:18; Deut 4:31; Deut 5:10; Deut 7:9; Ps 36:7–9; Ps 68:5–6; Ps 71:5–6; Ps 103:2–5; Ps 107:41; Ps 145:14–16). As Paul states, God will "make known the riches of his glory upon vessels of mercy" (Rom 9:23).

Again, when God wills to be gracious and compassionate with that deeper love that thoroughly saves a person from the power and guilt of sin, and brings him near for intimate spiritual fellowship with himself, he opens himself and *gives of his personal presence* "with all of his heart and with all of his soul" (Jer 32:36–41). God "marries" himself to those whom he wills to bring near to him in a true lasting spiritual relationship (Hos 2:19–20). He causes their hearts to regard him as their "portion" above all life (Ps 16:5; Ps 73:26; Ps 119:57; Ps 142:5; Lam 3:24). The prophets have always rested in this foundational character of Yahweh (Ps 86:15; Ps 103:8; Ps 108:4; Ps 145:8; Neh 9:17; Isa 55:6–7; Jer 31:1–3, 9–14, 18–20, 25; Joel 2:13; Jonah 4:2). This teaching is maintained in the NT (Rom 2:4; Rom 9:22–24; Eph 1:6, 12, 14; 1 Pet 2:9; 2 Pet 1:3; 1 John 3:1).

Blood Sacrifice

The sacrificial offering of animals to a deity was not unique to the He- brews, and the Torah records that it was the custom of the early Sem- ites and the Patriarchs to offer blood sacrifices to God (El Shaddai), for both sin atonement and thanksgiving (Gen 8:20; Gen 12:7; Gen 13:18). It seems entirely reasonable to assume that God had certain animals killed for the making of skins to clothe Adam and Eve in the garden (Gen 3:21). He eventually commanded regulated blood sacrifices for sin, for sanctifi- cation, and for gratitude through the Levitical priesthood (Exod 29; Num 18:1–7), coinciding with the establishment of the Mosaic covenant with the Israelites.

During the incipient period in the wilderness, God declared the divine concernment regarding the importance of the blood sacrifice and how the blood itself was to be revered as that which represented the very life of the animal victim (Lev 3:17; Lev 7:26–27; Lev 17:10–14; Deut 12:16, 23–24). The blood was regarded as the presence of the "soul (spirit) of the flesh," or, life-principle in a living being, as God states, "For the life of the flesh is in the blood" כי נפש הבשר בדם הוא (Lev 17:11). And God appointed this animal life-principle to be vicariously sacrificed for the covering of man's own life-principle, that he may be forgiven and spared of his life, stating, "and I have given it to you on the altar to make atonement for your souls" נתתיו לכם על־המזבח לכפר על־נפשתיכם ואני (Lev 17:11).

In doing so, God reveals the necessity of such a profound and disturbing sacrifice to effect atonement and forgiveness for personal and national sin, in that the animal stood in the place of the man that should, in fact, die for his transgression against the holiness of God. Once the person or people understood that the slaughter of the animal victim was to be the *substitute* for the person or people offering it, then it should be also perceived that *forfeiting of life* is the price for the evil done. The Torah certainly teaches the principle of divinely authorized *vicarious atonement* for sin. Even Moses, during the golden calf episode, astonishingly offers to have his own life terminated in the place of the rebellious Israelites. But his offer was not accepted because it was not authorized by Yahweh (Exod 32:30–34). We shall see, however, that there was eventually a human sacrifice authorized to die vicariously for the people.

Blood sacrifice was required for sanctification and atonement of both persons and things used in the service of Yahweh (Exod 29; Lev 4–6). However, with the worshiper's offer of animal sacrifice, there must be sincere feelings appropriate for the ritual; there must be both true sorrow and repentance for transgressions (Ps 32:5; Ps 51:1–9; Isa 1:16, 19; Isa 55:7), or there must be real gratitude for a thanksgiving offering (Ps 43:1–4). The offering should be preceded by a profound reverence for Yahweh, and the worshiper must have a deep-seated delight in the law of God so as to desire to be pleasing to him—all the more so after a particular transgression is repented of and atoned for.

These spiritual attitudes, accompanied with a striving after obedience, are necessary toward rendering the sacrificial offerings acceptable to God. But if these are not the true feelings of the offerer, then they are merely insulting to God. So then, if these genuine religious attitudes are lacking, God would be offended and resent the empty procedures—despite any formal correctness and religious propriety—as he has warned through his prophets throughout Israel's biblical history (1 Sam 15:22; Ps 40:6–8; Ps 51:16–19; Isa 1:10–17; Amos 5:21–23).

That a man's own life is, in principle, the real price for sin against God, but that animals were graciously substituted for him, can be seen in the *Akedah* event of the Abrahamic narrative, where Abraham is commanded to offer up Isaac, his only son, as a burnt offering (Gen 22:1–2). It seems an inescapable conclusion that God had *nearly required a human sacrifice* to be offered up, but that he had graciously desisted and instead had himself provided an animal in the place of Isaac.

The real requirement of the justice of our holy God for the violation of his holy law is the death of the sinner himself. This judgment is affirmed by the facts of the condemnation of Adam and Eve in the garden for disobedience, who would "surely die" (Gen 2:17), and the wrathful declaration of Yahweh to Moses that the sinner would be "blotted out of the book of life" (Exod 32:33).

This truth is also underscored by the fact, in the *Akedah* narrative, of how God had provided a ram to be offered up as a burnt offering "in the place of his son" (Gen 22:13). The general typology of bloody deaths of vicarious sacrifices commanded by Yahweh also points to this truth. The many recorded judgments of the Israelites being "cut off," sometimes meaning killed, in the Pentateuchal narrative are startling reminders of this divine judgment for sin.

Moreover, this fact of the forfeiture of life for sin is amazingly affirmed with the prophetic description of the Servant of Yahweh, who was *appointed to suffer death for the sake of the people of Israel*—for God visited the iniquity of Israel upon him. The prophet states, "the Lord has caused the iniquity of us all to fall on him" ויהוה הפגיע בו את עון כלנו (Isa 53:6). The prophet used unmistakable language, such as, he was "led as a lamb to slaughter," "by oppression and judgment he was taken away," "he was cut off out of the land of the living," "he rendered himself a guilt offering" אשם, and "he poured out himself unto death" (Isa 53:7–8, 10, 12).

The Servant is certainly *a distinct individual* from the people of Israel because he is described as the "Righteous Servant" in whom "there is no injustice" (Isa 53:9, 11), whereas the people of Israel are certainly described according to their unrighteousness and transgressions (Isa 53:5–6). He is certainly distinct from the nation of Israel because he is specifically commissioned to *restore* the people of Jacob, as well as to be a light to the nations (Isa 49:6). He is certainly distinct from the people of Israel because he is *abhorred* by that very nation (Isa 49:7). With the gracious self-offering of the Servant of Yahweh, he both satisfies the divine justice and effects vicarious atonement by his death (Isa 53:11). Whereas animals usually take the place of the repentant offerer, here, the Servant takes the place of the animal to be slain for the sake of the many who repent (Isa 53:6–7).

It must be reiterated and considered with all reverence that El Shaddai, the God of the Hebrews, had nearly required from Abraham *a human sacrifice*, but that later from himself he offered up, in the person of the Servant of Yahweh bearing the guilt of others' sin, the human sacrifice that his justice demands in order to offer forgiveness and reconciliation. The prophet perceives clearly that, in both of these situations, God had graciously provided the animal that was needed for an offering. He had provided, in Abraham's case, another animal in the stead of Isaac (Gen 22:8, 13), and he had provided a "lamb," in the person of the Servant, who was led as it were to slaughter (Isa 53:7). This is the *unmistakable message* that the prophet reports, yet it remains doubtful that many will believe it (Isa 53:1). This teaching is maintained in the NT (Matt 20:17–19; Luke 18:31–33; John 1:29; John 3:14–15; John 10:11–18; Rom 3:25; 1 Cor 5:7; 2 Cor 5:21; Eph 1:7; Heb 9:11–22; 1 Pet 1:2, 19; 1 Pet 2:24; 1 John 1:7; Rev 1:5).

The Ministry of the Holy Spirit

During the wilderness wanderings, when Moses is perturbed that he is overwhelmed with the management of the large congregation of Israel, Yahweh decides to put his same Spirit upon seventy elders along with Moses (Num 11:16–17). Moses subsequently exclaims the wish that all of Israel would be given the Spirit in them in order that they would all serve Yahweh as faithfully as a prophet who had God's Spirit influencing him: "Who would give the people of Yahweh (as) prophets, that Yahweh will put his Spirit upon them?" (Author's translation.) יהוה את־רוחו עליהם ומי יתן כל־עם יהוה נביאים כי־יתן (Num 11:29).

Both the fact of God's putting his Spirit upon the elders to serve Moses faithfully, and the wish of Moses that all of Yahweh's people would be given his Spirit to change and influence them to serve him rightly—even as a prophet of God—discloses the fundamental necessity of the gift and ministry of the Spirit of God to *change and empower* those who would be his faithful people. If the people whom Moses complains of were able, of their own natural soul, to love and serve Yahweh faithfully as he required, then there would be no point in the wish of Moses that they be given the Spirit.

The text refutes the notion that sinful man can devote his heart and life in true spiritual service to God. He must be enabled by the supernatural power of the Spirit of God. The accounts of the prophetic writings in the Bible are replete with the fact of the necessary ministry of the Spirit influencing the godly. The biblical writers reveal in various terms that the Spirit of God is the sole sovereign agent in supernaturally changing the evil heart of a man to love and fear the living God, acceptably and in truth. At times, it was for a temporary transformation of character for his secret purposes, but normally, it was for the permanent transformation that accompanies real salvation (Judg 3:10; Judg 6:34; 1 Sam 10:6–7; Isa 44:3; Isa 54:13; Isa 59:21; Jer 31:33–34; Ezek 37:5, 14; Joel 2:28–29).

The Spirit of God *implants, strengthens, and sustains holy desire for the will of God* as revealed in his word (1 Kgs 8:58; Ps 119:36; Isa 32:15; Isa 61:11; Zech 12:10). He enables the saved person to truly experience and intimately know God (Isa 54:13; Ezek 39:29). The Spirit's work in powerfully influencing the soul, whether for permanent salvation or temporary service, is secret and unasked initially, as we see in the case of Eldad and Medad (Num 11:26–29). The natural concomitant to the enabling of the Spirit of God, in the sinners' transformation, is the *divine determination to preserve this new spirit* toward God throughout the redeemed person's remaining days of natural life. They are kept by the Spirit through the same supernatural power that first gave them a heart that would be drawn near to God in sincere faith and love.

By the very nature of the divine implanting, or the sovereign invasion, of the "seed" of the principle of love for God in the redeemed person's heart—that comes not from the barren soil of their own spiritually dead soul but by the donation of divine grace—*it remains and persistently influences the character* of the man by the support and cultivation of the Spirit of God who implanted it (1 Sam 2:9; Ps 125:1–3; Jer 32:38–39; Ezek 36:25–27). Moreover, it is the Holy Spirit who spiritually "anoints," that is, he enables and impels a person for a special commission or office (Isa 61:1). The Holy Spirit might also be grieved by stubborn disobedience (allowed in divine providence) to the point that God will chastise and punish, even as an "enemy," those who do (Isa 63:10). This teaching is maintained in the NT (John 1:13; John 3:5–8; John 6:45, 63; John 14:16–17, 26; John

16:8, 13; Acts 1:8; Rom 8:2, 11, 16, 23, 26; 1 Cor 2:9–15; 1 Cor 6:19; 1 Cor 12:3, 11; 2 Cor 3:6–11, 17–18; 2 Cor 13:14; Gal 4:6; Gal 5:5, 16–18, 22–25; Eph 1:13–14; Eph 2:18–22; 1 Thess 1:5; 2 Thess 2:13; Titus 3:5; Heb 9:14; 1 Pet 1:2; 1 John 4:13).

The Love That God Deserves

The entire heart of man is absolutely and necessarily involved in the love that God requires from man; and Yahweh never was, and will never be, satisfied with perfunctory performances of his will stipulated in the covenant codes (Deut 6:5; Deut 10:16). God deserves to be loved, not merely the respect that arises from a sense of duty according to reason and conscience, but with "all of the heart, and with all of the soul, and with all of the mind" בכל־לבבך ובכל־נפשך ובכל־מאדך.

In the *Shema,* the love required for God is stated with a curious heaping of terms to emphasize the complete claim on our respect and affection. The last clause reads literally: "and with all of the uttermost of you" (Author's translation.) ובכל־מאדך (Deut 6:5). That is, love God without being able to find more of the heart to give him. Such is the goal of the command.

Love for God does not mean merely studying his scriptures to know things about him but to actually hold him dear in the whole heart so as to adore and serve him well: to enjoy his laws and lordship, to delight to fear him, to pursue him spiritually, and to humbly fear to dishonor him with displeasing behavior of life (Deut 10:12; 1 Sam 15:22–23; Neh 1:11; Ps 119:14; Hos 6:6).

To love God with the whole heart is to regard him as the only being of importance and the most important possession in life, and that the real and personal relationship of mutual love with God is as all wealth and blessedness, even as the greatest "portion" in life (Ps 16:5; Ps 73:25–28; Ps 119:57). Healthy love also involves an aspect of fearing to displease the beloved one. The dullness of our sinful spirits before God prevents us from being able to sharply appreciate either the love or the fear that is really due to God for either our redemption from guilt or the offensiveness of our sins even as redeemed servants (Ps 76:7; Ps 90:11; Ps 103:2–5, 8–12).

It is not the culture and ritual of formal religion but the possession of honest and personal fellowship that is biblical love for God. A man can pretend to serve God with exact and perfunctory ritual and yet be entirely estranged from the living God (Isa 29:13). God jealously examines the heart, expecting the sincere love and honor that he deserves (Ps 7:9; Jer 7:23–24; Jer 11:20; Jer 12:3; Jer 17:10). This understanding should be sufficient to eliminate any suggestion that the stupid coercion or compulsory devotion of false religions is to be regarded as a true characterization seriously worthy of the true God. This teaching is maintained in the NT (Matt 22:37; Mark 12:30; John 8:42; John 14:21, 23; John 15:9–10; Rom 8:28; Rom 12:1–2; 1 Cor 16:22; 2 Cor 6:17–18; Eph 4:1–3; Heb 13:15–16, 21; 1 Pet 1:17; 1 John 2:4–5; 1 John 3:3; 1 John 5:3).

Man Lives By God's Word and Will

When Yahweh let the rescued Hebrews hunger to the point of alarm and distress in the wilderness, and they were compelled to seek his help, he then decreed that the mysterious substance of "manna" should appear for their food. In this experience, God taught Israel that it is not enough that they have material well-being, but that all that God decrees, and every expression of his divine concern, and all the words that he utters (and implied through all this communication is the matter of his personal presence), were also to be important to man during his life, saying, "man does not live by bread alone, but man lives by everything that proceeds out of the mouth of Yahweh" עַל־כָּל־מוֹצָא פִי־יהוה (Deut 8:3).

Man lives or depends upon everything that proceeds out of the mouth of God as if it were veritable food and drink. His whole worldview and philosophy of life is to be molded and suffused with the *directives and reality portrayed by God's express declarations.* God is invisible, but by his divine omniscience his gracious depiction of reality is clearly revealed. An inescapable reality of the created order of mankind is the fact that true life-satisfaction comes only by the loving communion of one who is in fellowship with the Creator, and that all worldly concerns and interests apart from God will leave one unsatisfied (Isa 44:3–5; Isa 55:1–3; see John 6:49–51; John 7:37–38).

His word is to be received with absolute reverence and deeply cherished, and all his true devotees who have knit their spirits to God, will invariably do so (Deut 6:6; Deut 11:18; Deut 33:3–5; Josh 1:8; Ps 119:14, 20, 24, 35, 40, 49, 88, 94, 129, 159, 173). Because God, who ever lives, has faithfully depicted truth and reality, righteousness and justice, it is impossible that his word—the vehicle of this depiction—would ever perish (Isa 40:8). That which God has revealed he will do is certain to happen (Isa 14:24–27; Isa 43:13; Isa 45:23; Isa 55:11). It is an evidence of a man who truly belongs to God that he "trembles," or takes utterly seriously, all that God has said, never slighting it or transforming it to say what a man wants it to say (Isa 66:2). It is the surest barometer of sin, to deviate from the revealed will of God (Dan 9:5–6, 10–13). This teaching is maintained in the NT (Matt 4:4; Luke 4:4; John 8:31–47; 1 Thess 2:13; 2 Tim 3:16–17; Heb 1:1; Jas 1:19–25; 1 Pet 2:2; 1 John 2:4–5; Rev 1:3; Rev 22:18–19).

The Recognition of Moral Inability

Love from the whole heart for Yahweh was not attained with the majority of Israel, who needed such a loving heart toward God to fulfill the covenant and be blessed. And according to the revelation in Torah, that unless there was the granting of such sovereign grace and the necessary work of the Holy Spirit on the human heart, there would be none who would attain to such a disposition. This fact is shown by Yahweh uttering the profound question: "Who will give such a heart to them, one that is fearfully obedient, so that they would always fear God and keep his commandments?" (Author's translation.) מי־יתן והיה לבבם זה להם (Deut 5:29; see Exod 32:22; Deut 9:7–8, 22–24).

The language of this significant rhetorical question is very telling concerning the fearful necessity of a supernatural change of heart; that such a heart was not naturally found in the people of Israel. If Yahweh must wonder who would give the people such a conditioned disposition, then they themselves evidently could not produce it. The language refutes the opinion that man can turn his heart by his natural moral ability. Moreover the prophets categorically deny it, and the heart of sinful man is described as so deceitful that it would be impossible for him to perceive the true condition of his sinful disposition without the conviction of the Holy Spirit (Josh 24:19; Jer 17:9). This teaching is maintained in the NT (Matt 16:17; Luke 24:25, 45; John 1:5, 10, 13; John 3:3, 5–6, 19; John 6:44, 65; John 8:34, 44; John 10:26; Acts 7:51, 53; Acts 28:25–27; Rom 3:9–18;

Rom 7:7–14; Rom 8:3, 7; 1 Cor 2:14; 2 Cor 3:14–15; Gal 5:17; Eph 2:1–3; 1 John 1:8).

A Prophet Like Moses

When Moses warns the Israelites not to listen to the pagan practitioners of spiritism that they would encounter in the land of Canaan, he then tells them that God will raise up a prophet like himself from among their fellow Hebrew countrymen to speak on his behalf for their direction (Deut 18:14–19). It is to the divinely-commissioned Hebrew prophet that the Israelites are to give heed and reverence, and obey as though God had spoken directly to them (Deut 18:18–19). He will be like Moses in that he will speak in the name of Yahweh and communicate directly and infallibly the will of God for the people, as can be seen by the following context (Deut 18:20–22).

The passage is not necessarily saying that a prophet shall be exactly like Moses according to the magnitude of his calling in glory and wonders, despite the fact that during the Second Temple period there had developed the notion and expectation that a prophet having very much the caliber and majesty of Moses would eventually appear. His uniqueness and magnificent stature is established in his brief obituary toward the end of the Torah (Deut 34:10–12). Rather, this text is saying that future prophets shall be raised up who will have divine authority to be obeyed, as is evidenced in what Moses himself says should be done; that is, to "listen" to the true prophet, since it is what God "commanded him to speak" (Deut 18:15, 18). These true sent prophets were men who, by the influence of the Spirit, "stood in the council of the Lord," so that they saw and heard his word (Jer 23:18).

There were certainly other prophets who almost matched the glorious stature of Moses, such as Samuel and Elijah (Ps 99:6; Jer 15:1; Mal 4:5). It seems evident, however, that the basic concept of a sent spokesman for God having his delegated authority is what was in the mind of Moses, because it was not Moses himself whom God said to Malachi that he would send to restore Israel's relationships, but it was Elijah (Mal 4:4–6). Now, this declaration of further prophetism refutes the opinion that the divine revelation found encapsulated within the Torah is final, or that only the Torah is divinely inspired in such a manner that it alone must be heeded, and that the other scriptures of the Tanakh are inferior to it. The Torah itself refutes the notion that divine revelation is delimited to itself. Rather, there was yet to be further revelation announcing new things, spoken through the prophets whom God will have raised up.

There was yet to be further revelation, but only through the prophets that God would send to Israel. There was yet to be further revelation spoken through the Hebrew prophets, which shared the principle of authority that Moses had. This, then, is the basis for the awe, reverence, and obedience that the rest of the Tanakh deserves. And, as it has turned out, God had much more to say that develops the core ideas found within the Torah (Amos 3:7). This teaching is maintained in the NT (Matt 23:29–37; John 1:21; John 5:46; Acts 2:30; Acts 3:22–26; Acts 7:37; Acts 26:22; Eph 2:20; Heb 1:1; Jas 5:10; 1 Pet 1:10–12).

The Sovereign Privation of Necessary Grace

God sovereignly *withheld* such a heart that would rightly appreciate the grace and goodness shown to Israel. Moses declared to all Israel, "Yet to this day the Lord has not given you a heart to know, nor eyes to see, nor ears to hear" לכם לב לדעת ועינים לראות ואזנים לשמע עד היום הזה ולא־נתן יהוה (Deut 29:4). In Moab, Moses briefly recounted the great grace and power that Yahweh had shown toward Israel in their exodus from Egypt, their formation as a covenanted people, and many deliverances and provisions up until that time; yet they were not rightly appreciating these things so as to be compelled from the heart to love and serve God permanently. The appropriate spiritual response was dependent upon a supernaturally changed heart—a change Yahweh had withheld all that time.

God's determination to *withhold transforming grace* from many is undoubtedly one of the concealed and difficult to understand purposes that will be defended by Moses later in this chapter (Deut 29:29). The significant revelation in the fourth verse is important in that it refutes the supposed ability of man to freely decide to love and serve God with all the heart and permanently. A completely free moral will is the cherished opinion of traditional Judaism and the great majority of modern Christianity, which opinion cannot be reconciled to this disclosure.

Moreover, the text does not mean to say that this spiritual enabling was only withheld until that day, but that then God had provided such an enabling. No. The emphasis is on the not-giving of this grace לא־נתן, and there is no subsequent mention of a provision of the enabling within the context of this passage. The erroneous interpretation is also refuted by the facts that Moses will predict their certain defection from God and their punishment (Deut 29:22–28; and see Deut 31:14–22); Moses will compose a song of indictment for their certain condemnation and the vindication of God's wrath (Deut 32:1–43); and the subsequent disappointing history of Israel during the biblical period for the great majority of them.

This fearful fact of God's sovereign character has already been seen with his determined hardening of Pharaoh's heart to ensure his stubbornness toward Yahweh just so that he could display his powerful signs toward Egypt (Exod 4:21). Even after the children of Israel are shown grace and granted deliverance from Egypt, they are so untransformed that God's verdict is confirmed toward them that they, as all mankind, are basically an evil people (Num 14:27, 35, 43; see also Ps 78:32; Ps 81:11–12). The prophets recognize the divine privation of grace and the abandonment to a sinful disposition (Ps 81:12; Isa 63:17; Isa 64:7; Jer 2:19). This teaching is maintained in the NT (Matt 11:25; Mark 4:11–12; John 12:37–40; Acts 28:25–27; Rom 9:18; Rom 11:7–10, 25; 1 Thess 5:9; 1 Pet 2:8).

The Defense of God's Dealings with Mankind

Another profound disclosure that is embedded within the midst of the chapters on the blessings and curses, and the prediction of the apostasy of Israel and their punishment (Deut 28–32), is the statement that "concealed" purposes and dealings that are difficult to understand הנסתרת are God's concern, but the "revealed" and commanded matters הנגלת are the concern of the people (Deut 29:29). This verse is essentially a defense of God's sovereign purposes that will be seen to be non-understandable (particularly the withholding of necessary grace), while man's humility before God requires his concern toward the prescribed will of God for their lives, if they were willing to be obedient.

The perspective of scripture is that God deals with the whole mass of sinful man as a potter with clay fashioning a portion for his honor but leaving the rest for common use. The potter is perfectly righteous in these proceedings. God fashions some of sinful man, such as the Hebrews, to be a holy people for his glory, while leaving the rest to their dishonorable existence. Or God may choose to use a person for his purposes, though he does not have a saving relationship with him. Or, according to the forgoing context of chapter 29, he may destroy another people in wrath against their sinfulness and not offer mercy to them as he had to the Hebrews. Or he may severely punish some of the Hebrews for rebellion and not show mercy. What is clearly evinced from the rest of the Bible is that the fundamental reason that God is inherently just in such dealings is that, since all men are depraved in principle and would only hate God as they encounter him, no one has a claim on his love and protection, the offended one.

This verse, however, seems to more particularly address the Israelites' concern about how God dealt with them as a people. Moses seems to be saying that though they will observe sovereign dealings that are difficult to accept, still they are graced with knowing the redemption and will of God for those who will be happy to be his people. These redemptive blessings are all that really matters for their good, and they have this treasure forever. The defense of the divine sovereignty is the teaching of the prophets (Isa 29:16; Isa 45:9: Isa 64:8; Jer 18:1–6). This teaching is maintained in the NT (Matt 11:25–26; Matt 24:36; Acts 1:7; Rom 9:19–23; Rom 11:33–36).

The Enunciation of Transforming Grace

Then there is the important declaration that reveals God's greater grace in determining *to realize his salvation in Israel through his supernatural power,* in giving the change of heart that is absolutely necessary to love God rightly. We have here, in this entire passage, an enunciation of transforming grace (Deut 30:1–10). This determination is not merely an offer of salvation, nor an appeal to the conscience only, as God had already done with Israel who was delivered from Egypt. Rather, it is the resolve to cause the salvation of his people by his power so that it is realized in their lives as genuine.

The *determinative* character of the whole passage from verse 1 through 10 supports this interpretation as a certain prediction of restoration that God himself will effect by his power and sovereign grace, which is contrary to some commentators who find here a conditioned or hypothetical situation proposed to the people of Israel. In verse 1, the word "when" is the arbitrary opinion of the translators. More importantly, there is no hypothetical language here. The Hebrew certainty particle, "that," or, "indeed" כִּי is used here and throughout this passage. The text then states that "all these things, the blessing and the curse," וְהַקְּלָלָה כָּל־הַדְּבָרִים הָאֵלֶּה הַבְּרָכָה, which were spoken of before, *will certainly befall Israel* as their experiences, using predictive words, "it will happen that they will come upon you" (Author's Translation.) וְהָיָה כִי־יָבֹאוּ עָלֶיךָ (v 1). Verses 3 and 4 have in mind the "curse" component, and verses 5 and 9 have in mind the "blessing" component.

The reality is that Moses prophesies both of the polar experiences of being definitively cursed and then definitively blessed will be Israel's in their salvation history. That is, they will sadly succumb to the disobedience that merits the curses solemnly threatened, but then they will be lovingly rescued with saving grace to be the devoted people that will merit the blessings promised. When there really is a hypothetical situation in mind, the Hebrew interrogative, "if" אִם, would be used, as it is in verse 4—which actually does not admit of doubtfulness but assured recovery by any extent necessary despite Israel's geographical dispersion.

The most important declaration in this prophecy is that Israel will certainly turn to Yahweh "with all of their heart and soul" וּבְכָל־נַפְשֶׁךָ בְּכָל־לְבָבְךָ . . . וְשַׁבְתָּ (v 2). It is predicted as something God will effect by his power and grace because it includes both them and their children, which cannot be assured would happen if it was dependent upon their chance repentance. It will be effected by God's power because the very condition that God commands, love from "all the heart and all the soul," is what is promised by his power and grace in "circumcising their heart" in order that this disposition will be really present. He himself will "circumcise" their heart as well as their children, and not by themselves, "to love him with all the heart and with all the soul" לְבָבְךָ וְאֶת־לְבַב זַרְעֶךָ וּמָל יְהוָה אֱלֹהֶיךָ אֵת (v 6). The expression "uncircumcised of heart" means to have an *ineradicable contrary attitude* toward God. This is what is supernaturally corrected by God's grace (Jer 4:4; Jer 9:25–26).

So then, the very disposition needed to love God is effected by his power alone. Otherwise, there would be no need of this divine "circumcision," if indeed this disposition may be had by the people's own ability to change themselves. Then the grace promised would be meaningless, and the divine circumcision rendered redundant. Nor is it to be interpreted as some kind of extra-sensitizing of their heart upon their meeting the first conditions stated in verse 2 above, because if one can produce such a disposition within himself to begin with, then one can complete the work simply with greater effort on their part!

The subsequent context (vv 7–10) further confirms the predictive sense of this entire passage in that the statements continue to be empha-sized with the certain particle, "that," "for," "indeed" כִּי. Israel will cer-tainly turn, and listen, and keep the commandments with "all the heart and all the soul," which must be only by God's operation that makes it possible (v 6). This distinctive sense of the passage, regarding the impor-tant disclosure of supernatural grace that changes the heart of man, is confirmed throughout the Tanakh in the writings and preaching of the prophets. And though they utilize various metaphorical expressions of this grace, each one is always rationally reducible to the critical effect of a supernaturally changed disposition of the person's innermost feelings toward the things of God.

The expressions of the prophets are: the exchange of an evil, insen-sitive heart for a good, sensitive heart toward God and his will; or, the "giving" of a heart that will indeed fear and love God faithfully and per-sistently; or, it is the law of God being "put within" and "written" on the heart; or, it is being supernaturally "taught" by God (directly within the soul and not merely through the Levites, etc.); or, it is a "cleansing" by water; or, it is the giving a "new spirit"; or, it is a resurrection of a dead person (Isa 54:13; Jer 24:7; Jer 31:32–34; Jer 32:39–40; Ezek 36:25–27; Ezek 37:5–6, 12–14). The essential effects of this radical change of the heart are the *real presence* of both a persistent fear of displeasing God and the persistent sincere delight in the revealed will of God. That is, there is an empowerment to serve and love God, which is faithful and permanent (Ps 37:31; Ps 40:8; Ps 119:32, 36, 112).

The substance of this prophecy, that God will change the heart of those who will be saved, is the foundational revelation that supports later prophetic development, which describes the grace of the New Covenant provisions. This teaching is maintained in the NT (Matt 16:17; Luke 24:45; John 8:34–36; John 17:2, 6, 26; Acts 16:14; Rom 2:28–29; Rom 8:2, 9, 14; Rom 9:15, 18, 23; Rom 11:5; Gal 5:18; Eph 1:5–6; Eph 2:10; Eph 3:16; Phil 1:6; Phil 2:13; 1 Thess 1:4–5; 1 Thess 3:12–13; 1 Thess 5:9, 23–24; 2 Thess

2:16–17; 1 Tim 1:14; 2 Tim 1:7; Titus 2:11–12; Titus 3:5–6; Heb 13:20–21; 1 Pet 1:3–5; 2 Pet 1:3–4; 1 John 2:5, 20, 27; 1 John 3:9; 1 John 4:12, 19; 1 John 5:4, 18, 20; Jude 1, 24).

So then, the two core lessons of sin and grace can be abstracted from the foregoing profound teachings. They are the overarching themes of the Torah and are consistently alluded to throughout the rest of scripture. According to the regard of the holy prophets, and to Jesus and Paul, the Torah is the divinely sanctioned testimony of the grace of God toward Israel and their general failure to keep the covenant of grace granted to them; and then this whole Pentateuchal narrative serves as an augmenting context to concretely display the real power of sin in man's heart and the fearful necessity of supernatural help in order for redemption to be realized.

More than this, the saving grace that God wills to grant will be seen to be only a sovereign donation rather than a general expectation, and only through mediation that he himself will establish, beginning with the types and shadows of Moses and the temple service, and ultimately through the consummate atonement mediation of the sacrifice of Jesus the Messiah.

According, then, to this scriptural appreciation of the Torah, it is not correct to exalt the Torah above the rest of the Hebrew Bible because neither God intended it, nor the prophets regarded it, as elevated and separate but only as the principal controlling revelation upon which all later redemptive disclosure is developed.

6

Torah of the Sinful Nature

THE TORAH TEACHES, BOTH verbally and concretely, the fact of mankind's evil nature. It is one of the primary lessons of this great scroll, and an important matter of its teaching. Beginning with the Torah, the Bible presumes the fact that the "heart of man" is the innermost and real personality of any individual. His real and most sincere feelings about any matter are found here. The "heart" is the very seat of the affections and the thought life that necessarily involves the affections. When this part of a man has a certain disposition toward any object, there is no other secret part of his personality that will have a different disposition toward the same object. This, then, is the true state of his "heart" and it is his honest feelings. And so the biblical writers stress that the responsibility of man toward God should be with the sincerest feelings. God will have nothing less than the whole heart of one who professes devotion to him (Deut 6:5).

The particular evil characteristic that is an observable effect of the sinful nature is that of the "hardness of heart." This is a biblical metaphor that describes the phenomenon of *insensitivity* toward that which one should be appropriately concerned. This metaphor shows up the evil of the behavior in a way that is more accessible to the ordinary man. See for example Deut. 15:7. Hardness of heart is what is subjectively perceived by men.

But the Bible clearly reveals the objective fact of man's sinful nature despite what people think and feel about themselves, or the human race as a whole. This is a component of revelation through God's word, describing the totality of man's wickedness, which would not be naturally perceived or seriously assented to by fallen man. Still, this condition is not without its undeniable *phenomena* as just mentioned, which testify to this reality once this truth is apprehended by hearing the scriptures. The Torah, in accordance with its true teaching character, *demonstrates the reality* of mankind's universal depravity by two important empirical proofs: one situation involves a context without the advantage of the knowledge of true righteousness conveyed by means of a revealed law of God, and the other situation has the gracious advantage of the revealed law of God.

First, it can be seen to be true that mankind is *generally and frequently unloving and disharmonious* within itself; evil, in various measures, is certainly observed everywhere. This assessment is involved in the primary purpose of the opening chapters of the Torah (Gen 1–11), which are basically a polemic against the erroneous ancient pagan viewpoints of their gods and the creation of the world and man, which were rather optimistic concerning the general morality of humankind.

These chapters announce the facts of man's disobedience and consequent alienation from his Creator and the resulting moral chaos. It is asserted in the Torah: "Then the Lord saw that the wickedness of man was great on the earth and that every intent of the thoughts of his heart was only evil continually" (Gen 6:5). It is not merely the assessment of the author but the judgment of God that the depravity of man was rampant and thoroughgoing וירא יהוה כי רבה רעת האדם בארץ, and that there was to be found no truly good motivation stirring the heart of man in his character וכל־יצר מחשבת לבו רק רע כל־היום. And, "Now the earth was corrupt in the sight of God, and the earth was filled with violence. And God looked on the earth, and behold, it was corrupt; for all flesh had corrupted their way upon the earth." כל־בשר את־דרכו על־הארץ כי־השחית (Gen 6:11–12). And again after the judgment of the flood, God declares, "the intent of man's heart is evil from his youth." רע מנעריו כי יצר לב האדם (Gen 8:21).

Here, mankind's depravity is emphasized by the notice that the evil propensity is present and exhibited as soon as children consciously act for themselves. The divine assessment of man's basic evil nature found in these texts does not mean to describe humanity as only exhibiting continuous unkindness and selfishness among each other; rather, any good and natural behavior among sinful men is still only motivated ultimately by considerations that are *not induced by the love and honor* of the holy Creator of them, and so is assessed as evil in principle.

In these judgments, there is no room given to the false rabbinic notion of a remaining "impulse to good" יצר־הטוב in any true spiritual sense as just defined, much less a "divine spark" of goodness to be culti-vated among men. Such potential is positively denied by the later scrip-tures, even as an Ethiopian cannot change his skin color (1 Kgs 8:46; Ps 14:1–3; Ps 51:5; Ps 143:2; Jer 10:23; Jer 13:23; Jer 17:9)

Second, the sinfulness of man is proven within the momentous divine *experiment* of the formation of a covenanted people of God, the nation of Israel, who had been shown great mercy and given great privi-leges, and who yet had proved obstinate and rebellious toward God. God certainly has a right to, and did often, test the sincerity of the professed love of his worshipers by using the experiment of tempting or difficult situations (Gen 22:1–19; Exod 15:25; Exod 20:20; Deut 8:2, 16; Deut 13:3; 2 Chron 32:31; Ps 17:3; Ps 66:10–12).

It was the judgment of Moses that the redeemed Hebrew descendants of Abraham from Egypt and their establishment as a covenanted people of Yahweh was considered a *test,* or an experiment—especially during the period of the wilderness wanderings—to see if they would appreciate the grace and opportunity that they were given to prove their devotion to their redeeming God. Moses declared, "that he might humble you, test-ing you, to know what was in your heart, whether you would keep his commandments or not" לדעת את־אשר בלבבך התשמר מצותיו אם־לא למען ענתך לנסתך (Deut 8:2). Israel was supposed to bring glory to the one true God by their living for him alone (Isa 43:8–12). It was indeed a sincere offer of grace on Yahweh's part to make them his own beloved people, and he gave his love to them for the sake of their fathers (Deut 7:6–11; Isa 48:17–19). He would indeed love them and bless them if they would love him and keep his covenant.

This relationship would have been maintained. But since they were called by appeal to their *conscience alone* (that is, they were "taken by the hand") and not changed in their heart, concerning which we have seen is not owed by God, they then failed to honor the Mosaic covenant and so failed the test. The great majority (except a few elect ones) was not able to keep his commandments from sincere love and delight in the laws of his "way" (Ps 44:17–18). And even in the later Israelite history, only a relative few—an elect portion—were able to spiritually appreciate the grace of their calling (Isa 6:8–13; Rom 11:1–10). Israel was consequently a profound disappointment to Yahweh, according to the *song of indictment* of Moses (Deut 32:1–27).

The experimental nature of the Mosaic calling is proven also by the consideration of God's sovereign privation of the spiritual conditions needed to rightly appreciate the grace shown toward the congregation— the "eyes," "ears," and "heart to know" (Deut 29:4). God obviously knew their spiritual inability and yet required the people to love and obey him because it was their *moral responsibility* nonetheless. He obviously did not intend that this initial redemptive experience would be the thorough and everlasting salvation of his people that would be the praise and glory of his righteousness and holy name, as the prophets will yet announce (Isa 44:1–5, 21–23; Isa 54:13–14; Isa 62:1–5).

The gracious call of Abraham and his descendants, however, remains intact and will be realized throughout history by the secret and sovereign callings of individuals within that original calling; and Israel will be continually preserved and will yet come to experience national salvation in the latter days (Ezek 37:11–28), the timing of which development is known only to God (Rom 11:1–5, 25–27).

From another perspective, that of the ineffectiveness of the mere letter of the laws to cause righteousness to spring up with that genuine quality of love that only the Spirit can produce in the heart, the Mosaic covenant was seen to be *faulty* as a device to ensure the desired result of true spiritual salvation and devotion, specifically because of the distastefulness of its requirements to the sinful nature of the unchanged members of the people. It had to be displaced with a better and effective covenant. This is the "new covenant" that the prophets have announced, which will be discussed later (Jer 31:31–34; Ezek 37:26).

This need for a better covenant also proves the experimental nature of the Mosaic covenant at Sinai. After the new covenant is inaugurated with the coming of the Messiah Jesus and the giving of the Spirit to those who are called, the first covenant was regarded as the "old covenant," which only produced condemnation for those under its yoke (2 Cor 3:14).

During the encampment at the mountain of God in the Sinai desert, when Moses received the commandments and laws for holiness and the people had become so terrified by God's visible and sensational presence, they implored Moses to mediate for them. Yahweh was pleased with this request and then exclaimed the very telling statement in regard to the people, as discussed above. He uttered the profound question: "Who will give such a heart to them, one that is fearfully obedient?" (Author's translation.) מִי־יִתֵּן וְהָיָה לְבָבָם זֶה לָהֶם—so that they would always fear God and keep his commandments (Deut 5:29).

He is not merely well-wishing, as some translators have optimistically diluted the sense. Rather, he is emphasizing the real lack within the people, which cannot be provided by themselves or any other method apart from God himself. Yahweh is declaring that the genuine and spiritual fear that he requires is really not there in their heart and must be provided somehow. Yahweh, of course, asks this question rhetorically. But the point is surely that such a thing is absolutely necessary for this reverence to be actually realized with them; and that without the giving of such a heart within them, the seeming fear and devotion that they were then exhibiting during their awe before God's terrifying presence will not last, but will surely dissipate into hardness of heart.

Soon after Moses had received the covenant commandments at Sinai and the sons of Israel had publicly agreed to accept the terms, the people then resorted to measures, in the golden calf event, for proceeding without Moses. It was a form of rebellion, since it violated the divine requirements for Yahweh's pure worship (Exod 32:1–6). This insensitivity and affront to Yahweh's majesty and claims provoked his wrath, and he exclaimed with disgust that the people had "corrupted themselves" עמך כי שִׁחֵת, that they had "quickly turned aside" from his prescribed service סָרוּ מַהֵר מִן־הַדֶּרֶךְ, and that they were an "obstinate people" עָרֶף־הוּא עַם־קְשֵׁה (Exod 32:7–9).

Then after a long period of Israel being led through the wilderness and having lapsed many times into sinful murmuring, disobedience, and rebellions, when Moses and the Israelites had crossed the Jordan and Moses began his great speech in recounting the redemptive acts of Yahweh toward the people, he exhorted them to adopt the very attitude necessary to love and serve Yahweh for all his grace toward them. He commanded them, saying, "circumcise the foreskin of your heart" אֵת עָרְלַת לְבַבְכֶם וּמַלְתֶּם, and "stiffen your neck no more" וְעָרְפְּכֶם לֹא תַקְשׁוּ עוֹד (Author's translation.) (Deut 10:16).

By inference, this is another indication that a changed heart-disposition is necessary to love God in truth. As surely as there must be the cutting off of the foreskin to remove the covering of the male member, so there must be a removal of that which covers the heart and prevents the right responsive feelings of a man toward God. The natural result will be no more desire to spitefully disregard the will of God for their lives. This is what must be done, somehow, if they would be blessed in their relationship to God.

Yahweh declared to Moses the telling denunciation: "this people will arise and play the harlot," and again, "I know their intent which they are developing today" (Deut 31:16, 21). Then Moses in turn testified against them, "For I know your rebellion and your stubbornness; behold, while I am still alive with you today, you have been rebellious against the Lord; how much more, then, after my death?!" (Deut 31:27). Indeed, Moses was commanded to testify to the shameful sinfulness of Israel toward Yahweh's gracious dealings by composing the *song of indictment,* which he then recited to them, so that Yahweh would be vindicated of his punitive relationship with the people (Deut 31:27–30 and Deut 32:1–43).

In the "Song of Moses," which is actually Yahweh's indictment and witness against the people, Yahweh was declared perfectly righteous in all his relationship with Israel (Deut 32:3–4). God unashamedly declared its purpose: "in order that this song may be a witness for me against the sons of Israel" למען תהיה־לי השירה הזאת לעד בבני ישׂראל (Deut 31:19). In his unsought goodness and mercy, Yahweh made, established, and conceived these "sons and daughters" of the Israelites who were descended from their Hebrew fathers, with whom he first graciously established a covenant to be their God (Deut 32:6–10, 18).

Though the Hebrew descendants groaned as slaves in Egypt, they did not seek to initiate a covenant to be God's special people; this was God's plan. They did not even worship God (known then as El Shaddai), while enslaved in Egypt, but worshiped other gods (Josh 24:14). They alone of all the nations were made his special people and "the portion" in which he would be satisfied (Deut 32:7–9). But because of the sinful nature of the humanity of Israel, they then succumbed to the evil insensitivity of their hard hearts; they in turn spurned God and rejected the gratitude, devotion, and obedience that God naturally deserved (Deut 32:5–6, 15–18).

Because of God's goodness toward them in enriching the people with freedom, dignity, and prosperity, Israel became arrogant and slighting of their majestic benefactor; "Jeshurun grew fat and kicked" (Deut 32:15). The later records, following the initial events of the Torah, which recount the subsequent historical experiences of the people of Israel, are mostly the sad and wearisome accounts of the sinful backslidings and spiritual infidelities of Israel and Judah.

Later also, God raises up the Prophetism that is so well known with their solemn reactive tasks—being thoroughly versed, impelled, controlled, and bounded by the original divine instructions of the Torah—of rebuking Israel and Judah for their sins and infidelity. Involved within these reactive messages of the prophets were many descriptions and pictures of the particular sins, disobediences, and idolatries that were committed by the people throughout the many centuries of the biblical period. And so beginning with Moses and throughout this sacred history, we find recorded that the prophets indict the people, who were graciously called into covenant fellowship with God, as having rebelled and defected from this calling to "serve other gods."

After the initial covenantal failing of the golden calf incident, Yahweh was so offended that he considered destroying the entire congregation and starting fresh with Moses' lineage. But Moses implored Yahweh that he would put away his wrath, and reconsider both how they would look to the Egyptians as well as the promises made to their fathers. He begged that God would yet fulfill the promises to multiply the fathers' descendants and to give the land of Canaan to them. Moses' intercession was persuasive and God was moved to relent of his wrathful intentions (Exod 32:7–14).

Moses was graced by God and consequently beloved, and so his mediation was acceptable to Yahweh. Therefore, God was yet willing to go with him and the people to Canaan (Exod 33:12–17). God renewed the covenant, and stated that he would do even greater supernatural exploits than before (Exod 34:10). But the relationship that God sustained with Israel from that point forward was, as it were, only a *quasi-covenant*. It was mostly one-sided, for God's part, and imperfectly kept, for Israel's part. Moses acknowledged that the people were "stiff-necked"; that is, *not compliant* with the covenantal demands. Still, he begged God to be tolerant and forgiving and to yet fulfill covenantal promises toward them (Exod 34:9).

As can be seen from the rest of Israel's history, their relationship with God was characterized by a continual stream of divine appeal, tolerance, rebuke, punishment, and reconciliation. It was rarely one of rejoicing and resting in the divine favor due to covenantal fidelity. The renewed Mosaic covenant came with *warnings* (Exod 34:9–27), whereas the new and better covenant, as we shall see later, came with *certainty*. Though God continued to treat Israel as his inheritance, this *national mercy* came with the sorrowful evaluation of both Yahweh and his spokesmen, that the people are *not able* to serve him and will continue to violate the covenant because they are really evil in disposition, and God is holy (Deut 31:16, 20, 27, 29; Josh 24:19).

So then, one of the great secret purposes that were intended for the Mosaic covenant-experiment of Israel's calling was to *concretely demonstrate* the sinful nature in man, and how it is provoked and proved to be his reality by the giving of the commandments for their holiness toward God. The deep conviction of this shameful and hateful characteristic of man is necessary, and is sovereignly applied to the redeemed person's conscience by the work of the Holy Spirit in order for that man to appreciate the grace of God in genuine spiritual salvation. This purpose is the understanding of Jesus and Paul in the New Testament scriptures (Matt 5:17–20; John 1:17; John 3:19–20; John 5:45; John 7:19; Rom 7:5, 7–13; 2 Cor 3:6; Gal 3:19).

7

Torah of Divine Grace

The thrust of this book's message is that the Torah reveals these two core truths: that mankind is utterly sinful without the influence of the Holy Spirit, and that God must change a man first in order for him to be saved from divine damnation and restored to spiritual fellowship with God. The commandments are rather subservient in that they serve the purpose of exposing the sin of unredeemed man, but then serve as the rule of righteousness for the redeemed man who does wish to serve God.

The second core truth will now be demonstrated more fully. The "instruction" of divine grace, which stems from the foundational revelations during the Pentateuchal era, is providentially developed and clarified through a steady course of prophecy upon prophecy. And when all the prophets are carefully considered, the matter of God's grace proves to be rich with meaning, power, application, and glory.

There is nothing more important in the world than to be loved by God, because to be loved by God is the invaluable fortune of being the one who is the predetermined object, from before the foundation of the world, of God's purpose to be rescued from a life of sin and to be lovingly cared for throughout his endless existence. To be loved by God is to be one whom he has not passed over for salvation, but rather has been chosen to be graced with a heart to love God in truth when the rest of the world is left with their hatred for God. Then, in turn, God will further love this one with approving affection and delight because of the godly character formed in him.

And to have Yahweh as God is to be, in this manner, loved and protected both bodily and spiritually. God in his goodness gives to multitudes, the many millions throughout the ages who are not drawn by his sovereign will to be saved, various things to enjoy in this life; but to those whom he has set his love upon, he gives himself to enjoy forever. This is the fundamental distinction between the saved and the unsaved.

The Torah is clear that God sovereignly determines to set his love upon a particular person or a people who are found in their natural state of sinfulness. But the corollary is also true then, despite the trenchant popular convictions of both rabbinic Judaism and the Christian church, that God the Creator does not love all mankind in this manner just described. According to, firstly, the Torah and then all of the scriptures, the actual treatment of God toward sinful mankind apart from the redeemed and covenanted Hebrews is that of wrath, accursed estrangement, and divine repugnancy. We see this immediately after the rebellion of Adam and Eve in the Garden of Eden. God in his just anger curses their existence and then drives them from his holy presence; the settled attitude of divine resentment is depicted by their being barred with the flaming swords of the cherubim ensuring their estrangement as the just judgment for their disobedience (Gen 3:14–24).

Throughout the Torah, there are numerous examples of the people of Israel's unbelief and disobedience being met with wrath and being punished severely, as well as the unspoken settled wrath of God toward the surrounding pagans, which often becomes noticeable when the Israelites encounter them. They are not generally treated with lovingkindness but are usually judged and destroyed. The point is that God does not love the unredeemed with affection and approval. Rather, he justly hates them; and he says as much unashamedly through his prophets in his word (Ps 5:4–6; Ps 11:5). It is morally impossible for God to have loving affection or delight toward sinners; he would deny his own holy and inviolable character if he did feel warm affection toward such sinners. God cannot look with approval upon a sinner as such (Hab 1:12–13).

However, as is also evident from the Torah and the rest of scripture, God did not immediately destroy the actual existence of Adam and Eve after their sin but he continued to extend the mercies of preservation according to their created nature; he drove them away from his presence but did not destroy them (Gen 3:21, 23). Here then is the difference: according to man's moral nature he is absolutely hated, but according to his created nature, he is yet cared for in some measure. This is the sheer mercy of God's prerogative; it is lovingkindness that is undeserved. This distinction of the kinds of divine attitudes is reflected both in the prophets and the Apostles of the Lord Jesus. David unashamedly expresses this righteous hatred toward the wicked (Ps 15:4; Ps 26:5; Ps 119:113, 158; Ps 139:19–22); and the Apostles demonstrate their disgust toward the unrepentant (Acts 7:51–53; Acts 23:2–3; Acts 28:24–28; 1 Cor 16:22; 2 Tim 4:14). At the same time, there is required sincere kindness for the sinner's well-being as he is a fellow human being; there is shown love for their created persons (Deut 10:18; Matt 5:43–48).

In the Deuteronomy passage, Yahweh demonstrates his undeserved kindness in caring about the stranger's need for food and clothing, which proves no acceptance of their moral character. And with the teaching of Jesus in the gospel of Matthew, he is only repudiating that Jewish tradition that encouraged the kind of hatred for their enemies that involved unkindness and mistreatment to their persons, but he is not disallowing that holy hatred of the wicked person's moral character of which both God and his prophets have testified to, according to the passages we have seen already. This is surely the intention of Jesus as he underscores the kind of love for enemies he means when he points to the fact of God's undeserved yet shown love for the evil ones in causing the sun to rise upon them and sends the rain on the unrighteous as well as his beloved ones, because it is serving their created needs. This does not prove acceptance of their persons before him as they are plainly regarded as "evil" and "unrighteous," and are certainly under the wrath of God.

God will have us practice this *complex regard* for the unsaved around us, even as he regards man from a dual perspective both toward their created nature and their evil nature. We are to do good even to our enemies, that is, not intentionally mistreat them, demonstrating God's undeserved kindness and glorifying him through it (Luke 6:27–35). Though this should be sincere, we are not required to feel warm affection or delight for their repulsive spiritual character. This critical understanding of how God shows love toward sinful mankind is very helpful to rightly understanding the general message of salvation that is found in the New Testament, as well as the duty of the godly man toward the ungodly around him.

Since mankind is evil and continually offensive to the holiness of God, as we have learned from the opening portions of the great scroll of the Torah, and naturally deserving of wrath and judgment, then if God will do good and show love toward mankind, it must come in the form of grace, which is goodness toward someone that is not merited or deserved. The goodness is undeserved because we are naturally and persistently unrighteous, and it is not just to show love toward an unrighteous person according to the strict divine justice. Divine grace is the power of divine love *willing to overlook the dishonor* of behavior that clashes with God's holy character in order to freely show love toward an evil person, *giving the necessary goodness* of a changed nature, forgiveness, and justification for the acceptance of his person. It is God's sublime *goodness,* giving rise to his strong and immense love, that freely wills to do good toward a sinner, but it is his immense *creative power* that performs this necessary work in the life of that man.

God is clear and emphatic in his scriptures that it is the very same power that can create ברא the universe that can also *create* the spiritual conditions that are necessary for transforming the character of sinful man. It should be appreciated by us that when we see an insect, we cannot create it and put life into it and direct it to live according to its instincts, despite how hard we might wish or dream to be able to! And then we should extend this consideration of our human impotence to the entire world, and then we will approximate how mighty is God's creative power.

It is critically important to understand this point: it is God's glorious creative power that produces the salvation that the called ones are made to experience; that it is *not mere moral persuasion,* such as another man externally exhorting the conscience, that influences the man's mind to change his heart's attitudes toward the serious things of God. When Yahweh declared, in the Torah revelation, that he will "circumcise the heart" of those whom he intends to redeem, he also implied that it will be by his supernatural power because it was not to be found in the natural state of the heart of Israel (Deut 5:29 and Deut 30:6). And if God must do this work, then it cannot be possible of sinful man's ability. Also, Yahweh spoke to the people of Israel that when they were to come into the Promised Land through conquest, they were to appreciate the fact that all of the good things necessary for enjoying the land were already prepared in God's providence, and were not produced by their efforts. Because of this kindness of God in all the earth, they were to be sure to fear and love Yahweh always. This serves, no doubt, as a picture of the grace of God toward Israel in their spiritual need as well (Deut 6:10–13).

When David, one of Israel's truly redeemed and enlightened men under the old covenant era, expresses his repentance for his sinfulness, he also begs God to "create" ברא in him a clean heart, by which he means that Yahweh would strengthen him with an upright spirit (Ps 51:10). In his case, he had already been circumcised in heart, shown by the facts that he really loved Yahweh, and despite his lapse was repentant and wished to be renewed with strengthened devotion to be pleasing to God—dreading most of all the loss of the felt presence of God (Ps 51:10–13). He considered it to be only effected by that same power that Yahweh has to create anything at all. When God speaks of his spiritual salvation for those whom he loves, he brings near the fact that he is the Creator of the world and that this is a unique glory for which he is very jealous.

Jacob-Israel is comforted with the assurance that their deliverer is also the very "creator of the ends of the earth" בורא קצות הארץ, and so is very able to help his people who long for him (Isa 40:27–31). When Yahweh begins to speak of his determination to help Jacob-Israel, he declares that he will effect new geographical conditions that can only be accomplished by a power belonging to the Creator, to illustrate the marvelous quality of the salvation experience (Isa 41:17–20; see Isa 43:7, 15). This is to ensure that they confess that "the hand of the Lord has done this" and "the Holy One of Israel has created it" (v 20).

The divine determination to raise up a generation of devoted servants that will be truly righteous and strong in their walk before God is considered as the observable effect of the planting and growth of a tree. They are "the branch of my planting, the work of my hands, that I may be glorified" (Isa 60:21); and "they will be called oaks of righteousness, the planting of the Lord, that he may be glorified" (Isa 61:3). God has his inspired prophet declare the significant utterance that he will effect salvation and display divine righteousness (through Cyrus) as wonderfully and certainly as his created natural world produces fruit according its design, despite the impotence of mankind. Again, God asserts that this salvation will come about because of his power that "created" it בראתיו אני יהוה (Isa 45:8). The inspired writers of the Jewish New Testament well understood that the very same power to create the heavens and the earth is the same supernatural power that transforms the souls of redeemed men to have the faith and love toward Jesus the Messiah that is necessary for salvation (2 Cor 4:6; Eph 2:4–10; Eph 4:23–24; Col 3:10; Jas 1:18).

And so by metonymy, "grace" is also to be understood for *the divine power that is exerted* toward a man who has already found "grace" in the eyes of God; all the contemplated forms of God's unmerited goodness, such as "grace" חן, "lovingkindness" חסד, "compassion" רחם, "mercy," "favor," are so many expressions of that essence of goodness that is of the glory of God's interior. It is necessary that we understand these two distinct aspects of the matter of divine grace, both the kind regard and the exerted power, because it will help us to soundly appreciate the infinite value of the kindness that God gives to those individuals who are chosen to be rescued from the power and guilt of sin in their lives—to really "taste and see how good the Lord is" (Ps 34:8). We should rightly and intelligently appreciate all of the works that God exercises toward us so as to give him his due glory and not underestimate the gracious favor that he grants, so as to not rob him of glory and the proper love and gratitude that is his rightful due. As much as is in our individual power and character to do so, we should know and clearly understand all of the particular aspects that make up the collective grace of God toward us.

8

The Role of Faith in the Torah

THE TORAH REVEALS TO careful observation that faith is closely connected to this miracle of the change of the heart's moral affections in that it will immediately begin to operate and be exercised toward the revelation of God in the forms of belief, reception, and obedience. Why? Because the very condition necessary for a man to believe God is loving affection or respect, and this is precisely what is provided in this miracle of grace. If we are enabled to love God, we will inevitably delight in his biblically-described character and take seriously whatever he has to say. This is the very process of genuine faith.

There are two necessary components involved in the experience of biblical faith (which is to totally apply one's person to what is believed) for it to take place:

1. The content of revelation; or, the object of faith;

2. The moral "taste" for that content.

From the subjective standpoint, it is the moral taste that is critical, because if what is heard is not appealing to a person, then he may believe it to be factual but will never be drawn toward it. It is the component of moral taste that is graciously supplied in the heart of man for his salvation.

It is critically important to understand this point that the Torah clearly reveals: that before faith is possible, the supernatural change of the heart is what is *first* needed to take place in God's redemptive interaction with an individual in order for that person to respond favorably and reverently to God. Simply put, God must first change a person's heart before that person will turn to God for salvation. As we have seen in this study, God has disclosed that this is the most basic lack and the main problem with man's nature. This is why the Israelites did not believe Yahweh during the crossing of the wilderness. This is why the miraculous care of Yahweh did not induce the spiritual loyalty that it should have.

In the book of Isaiah, we have some of the strongest indictments regarding the falsehood of Israel's religion before Yahweh, as we have seen earlier. There we find the significant expression of Moses echoed, first uttered in the Torah, concerning the evil spiritual condition of the Israelites—that they were not given the "eyes," nor the "ears," nor the "heart," to spiritually appreciate Yahweh's grace toward them, and how they should love him in return for it (See Deut 29:4). These are obviously metaphors referring to the main physical means by which mankind perceives objective reality in natural life. With his senses, he sees things, and hears things, and understands things with his heart (or mind) that inform him of his objective natural circumstances. Isaiah alludes to it in regard to the people of Judah that they are astonishingly "blind" and "deaf," even spiritually "imprisoned" or "trapped in caves." The meaning is that they were spiritually impotent and unresponsive to Yahweh's grace in any truthful and pleasing way (Isa 42:18–22; Isa 48:8).

This miserable spiritual condition is theirs because of the sovereign decree of Yahweh to leave them to their evil natures (Isa 6:9–10). Yahweh, however, will demonstrate the *infinite value* of his sovereign grace by transforming a remnant of the people to be spiritually responsive so as to fear and love him in truth, by the giving the "eyes," and the "ears," and the "heart" (Isa 35:4–5; Isa 42:6–7, 16). And this remains the basic problem with the unbelieving Jews today. They have been greatly advantaged with the grace of God as described in the Torah, but the majority (those who reject the Messiah Jesus) has substituted an invented form of Judaism while disregarding the plain message of the prophets. They do not, or rather cannot, love God himself in an immediate, deep, personal relationship. This is evident by their disregard and disobedience to much of what Moses and the prophets taught. Rather, they have taken some of the things of God and his Torah, and developed an unauthorized and superficial culture based heavily upon the darkened teachings of their sages and rabbis, as God had complained about long ago (Isa 29:13).

It is the *culture* of rabbinic Judaism that is trusted in, delighted in, studied, upheld, and served, along with a distant lip-service to God and to the Tanakh. It is a fleshly apprehension and appropriation of the revelatory aspects that even an evil heart can admire in themselves. A sinful man can still respect qualities in another being that are naturally attractive and desirable to him—the power to create or change things, goodness to change things, mercy to help or forgive things, laws that regulate behavior among persons, etc. All these qualities that are found in the description of God in the Torah are naturally admirable and desirable as mere qualities in themselves. But this is a kind of reverence for the divine one's qualities for self-serving reasons, and therefore may come short of biblical love for God. When respect is held for the power, attributes, and revelation of God in the Bible, which is then utilized as an ostensible basis for the man-made, top-heavy construction of revered sayings and traditions of the sages and rabbis, which are in fact exalted above the priority and plain-sense revelation of the Tanakh, then there is no genuine honor for him. This knowledge of the Torah is thoroughly colored by the uninspired interpretations of the sages and rabbis.

To love God is not only to admire qualities that he possesses but also to be knit to him, and to desire and value his approval, delight, and lordship, and to love him for his whole person immediately, deeply, and personally. We must realize that he requires total respect and obedience for all his demands, specifically expressed through his ethical commands, and total respect and observation for all that he says, demonstrated through obedience to Moses and all the prophets. That is, the person who loves God is personally and entirely glad to belong to him, and be changed by him, and be submissive to his plain word; all of which is concisely stated with the beautiful expression of being "bound" or attached to God, even as one willfully commits himself to a beloved wife (Isa 56:3, 6; see Gen 29:34). It is to value him and be so satisfied with him as to feel there is no other importance in the world compared to him (Ps 73:25). And enjoying the biblically described love and approval of God toward one's person is all that ultimately matters in life (Ps 73:28). This is the essence of biblical faith.

Regarding a man's moral justification and the forgiveness of his sins before the Holy One, as we have already seen earlier, there are in the Torah a number of important verses that disclose the divine requirement of faith, or loving reliance, to be in a pleasing and right relationship with God. And we have seen that this involves reverently believing and honestly responding to all that God had said to believe and to do.

The foremost verse is the profound declaration, discussed earlier, that reveals that by believing God's revelation and promises, one would be accounted righteous (as Abraham had experienced) and this would be without regard to a man's moral efforts. It was not a justification due to

Abraham's practice of righteous living before God (which was certainly imperfect); rather, it was a free and gracious crediting of a righteous standing with God simply for lovingly believing what God has revealed to believe. This belief as a condition in itself could never make up for all the required righteousness that Abraham owed the Creator during his existence, and so this is not the ground or merit of Abraham's justification. But his justification was gifted to him upon this condition of wholehearted trust in the revelation of God.

And there are also the recorded divine statements that either express the nature of the trust and reliance that is demanded of the Hebrews, or the criticisms of their failure to be trusting and devoted to Yahweh (Gen 15:6; Exod 4:5; Exod 14:31; Num 14:11; Num 20:12; Deut 1:32; Deut 9:23). However, when God solemnly declares the radical problem with the unbelieving Hebrews, he does not merely state that they remain in an unconvinced frame of mind, or are not yet sufficiently persuaded. Rather, he discloses the fact of their heart needing to be transformed by such a profound change that only he can do to it, and this change necessarily involves the transformation of the affections (Deut 5:29; Deut 10:16; Deut 29:4; Deut 30:6). Let it not be misunderstood that the supernaturally changed heart is specifically what is mentioned as necessary for the man to love God and fear him rightly, with the implication being that *genuine faith will naturally follow.*

This salvific order (that grace precedes faith) is evident when we reconsider these preceding divine statements, as well as the commandments spoken to the congregation of Israel for their duty in the covenant. In reaction to the distrust and disobedience of the Hebrews, though Yahweh complains many times how they fail to believe him, he says pointedly that *the lack was the heart,* rather than faith (Deut 5:29). And by indicating the "heart," this means *the affections*—the innermost feelings of liking or enjoying something—are what are lacking, due to moral perversion. Again, when Yahweh commands the people to keep the covenant that he has provided them for their redemption, he requires "love from the whole heart," and *not merely belief* or intellectual acknowledgment. This involves the most sincere positive affections, the feelings being the final personal reference of approval or disapproval toward anything.

The affections are they which dispose the whole soul. It is morally impossible to disregard that which our feelings are bent toward, be it good or evil. So, if God has our heart, then our whole personality will serve him; this is what God deserves and commands in his word, and anything less is the same as not to love him (Deut 6:5). Therefore, it is love that God will put in the interior of a man, causing him "to love the Lord with all his heart and with all his soul," which will ensure the man's trust and obedience—the response of faith—so that he will certainly cling to God within his redeemed relationship (Deut 30:6).

The faith and devotion that is pleasing (and consequently justifying) in the sight of God, which is produced by the divine granting of his Spirit within men's spirits, is characterized by the *concise description* of a genuine godly person, found in Isaiah: it is the one who fears Yahweh in such a manner so as "to trust in him, and also obeys the voice of his servant"; that is the one who belongs to Yahweh so as to be able to regard him as "his God" (Isa 50:10). It is not to fear Yahweh alone *but also to obey his servant,* whoever and whenever that prophet has been commissioned to reveal the will of God, the principle of which is according to the forewarning of Moses (Deut 18:15, 18–19).

If the servant of God has not been obeyed, then God has not been obeyed, and then that relationship is proven false. God himself has indeed spoken, and also he has spoken through his servants, the prophets. And everything they have revealed to be believed and obeyed is as much as if God himself has spoken it. If a man pretends to fear God but disregards one of his servants who have been providently raised up and sent to the people, or if a man be selective about what he is pleased to pay attention to and spurn the rest of his prophecies, then he demonstrates that he is devoid of the Spirit's grace and does not really belong to God. This man is, in fact, disobedient. When the reality of the exile had come upon Judah, God declared that *their general disobedience to the prophets was disobedience to him* (Jer 29:19).

This is the basic error of the unbelieving Jews, historically and today. They do not understand or obey everything that is spoken by the prophets, however much they congratulate themselves for keeping the Torah. This principle, stated in Isaiah, was reiterated by the Messiah Jesus, who was himself the pre-eminent prophet or servant that God has raised up to be obeyed. His principle was concisely the same argument, that if someone was belonging to God, then they would have room in their hearts for his words (John 8:37–47).

Let it be clearly and seriously understood that if any man (Jew or gentile) wishes to belong to God, he must obey the words of the sent one,

Jesus the Messiah, according to the teaching of Moses in the Torah (John 5:37–47; 1 Pet 1:2; 1 John 3:23). And the deeper reason is because, as the later prophets more closely adumbrate, it is God himself who has come as the humble servant for the purposes of grace and redemption. And so, without dispute, he must be obeyed.

Again, we can see this principle, which was first enunciated by Moses and maintained by the prophets and by Jesus, being taught by John in his first letter where he discusses the "testing of the spirits" (1 John 4:1–6). They that know God listen to the Apostles whom he has sent (v 6). And when a speaker confesses convictions that are in accord to prophetic revelation, then it is proven that he is from God. Indeed, by this principle, one will even know the Spirit of God! That is, one will know that these whole-souled confessions are compelled by the true influence of the Spirit of God within him, because the important matter is whether one's faith and devotion are begotten by the Spirit of God (v 2). Again, one whose faith and devotion are produced by the influence of the Spirit of God is the one who overcomes the tyranny and prison of religious falsehood and self-deceit, because it is begotten by another and not of his deceptive and impotent heart alone (v 4).

9

The Further Prophetism Announces New Things

THE FOUNDATIONAL REVELATION OF the Torah records the intention of God, expressed through his servant Moses, that there was to be another prophet (or, other prophets) like Moses (Deut 18:15–19). The Torah is indeed the foundation, but it is just that, a foundation. And upon this revelatory foundation, God designed to build the sublime structure of his salvation. It was given to the later prophets to fully unveil this plan of salvation. It is the revealed will of God that there was yet to be other spokesmen who will yet disclose more of the mind and will of God to the people of Israel. This datum is very important and not to be despised, as God warns concerning the due reverence that he should receive through these future prophets (Deut 18:15, 18–19; see also Exod 23:21–22).

Besides the somber denunciations of Israel's deviation from the national covenant experiment, the essential burden of the later prophets was to disclose the *new things* that God had determined to effect by his power within the experience of his called people (Isa 42:9; Isa 48:6). In the book of Isaiah, we come upon the specific idea of "new things" חדשות (Isa 42:9; Isa 43:19; Isa 48:6) that God announces will come to pass by his sovereign power (Isa 46:8–11). One "new thing" was that God would deliver exiled Judah by making a "way" through the desert in a remarkable manner as he had done with Israel in making a way through the sea when he had delivered them from Egypt (Isa 43:16–21; see Jer 16:14–15).

But that Babylonian deliverance cannot be all that Isaiah means when he writes the words of Yahweh concerning his special servant that he will commission. Within the song of the calling and commission of the Servant of Yahweh are mentioned "new things" that will take place with the very coming of this anointed one. That is, "new things" are closely connected to, and inaugurated by, the appearance and the commission of the Servant of Yahweh (Isa 42:1–9; Isa 49:5–6; Isa 52:13–15).

In the song of the Servant, there is stated a definite purpose for this particular servant, accomplishing the remarkable new situation of a *true, spiritual, global knowledge and worship* of the one true living God (Isa 42:1–6). This universal worship of Yahweh, the true God, is termed the "judgment" and "teaching" and "light" that the Anointed One brings to the nations. Up until this time, Israel had only known the supernatural events and establishment of the national religion based on the Mosaic covenant, designated by the phrase, "the former things have come to pass." But now, there will be divinely ordered new events bringing about "new things"; divine interventions of which they were not accustomed to according to the former redemptive experience.

What these "new things" are can be ascertained by the new situations that God announces he will accomplish through the prophecies of the later prophets, which are radically different spiritual dealings with God's people than they had been accustomed to for centuries according to the structure of the old desert covenant with Moses. When the prophets announce new things to be accomplished by the sovereign power of God, it is with the understanding that Yahweh remains faithful to the original Covenant of Grace with Abraham and his descendants generally.

There is the underlying divine commitment to perpetually preserve and ultimately bless the distinguished Hebrew people with real spiritual salvation. There is yet a future for Israel. These new dealings are specifically and definitively connected with the coming of the anointed Servant of Yahweh. The principal "new things" that the prophets reveal consist of a new spiritual covenant, a new spiritual mediation, a new spiritual temple, a new spiritual Davidic kingdom, a new revelation of Yahweh, and a renewed world.

10

The New Covenant:
The Spirit Will Make the Believer

THE TORAH IS VERY clear that when God has determined within himself to grant the grace of salvation to a particular individual, he also determines to *actually save* that person in space and time, in actual history at some predetermined point of time and circumstances. He then puts forth at that appointed time supernatural power to change that elected person, for a change is absolutely necessary. The change required, simply stated, is to bring a man from hatred and disobedience toward God to a state of love and obedience toward him. As we have come to see from the foregoing study of the Torah, the natural and present state of every person's attitude toward God, whether young or old, is having the principle of hatred toward God, expressed and subjectively felt in varying degrees from indifference through strong detestation, resulting in the natural consequence of thorough and persistent disobedience to the will of God for their created lives. But it is the power of God's salvation to bring a person to the state of having a principle of love for God, resulting in sincere and persistent obedience, though not without imperfection. This is the essence of the New Covenant.

How then does God cause this critical change in a person's soul to take place? What exactly happens by God's power to effect this transformation? It has been briefly described earlier in this study, and will be elaborated here. There are various descriptions employed throughout the scriptures to help especially the believers to comprehend the significant divine operation that takes place. Such metaphors as: being given "eyes and ears" (Deut 29:4), being "circumcised in heart" (Deut 30:6), the law being "implanted" and "written" on the heart (Jer 31:33), being given a "singular heart" (Jer 32:39), being "implanted with the fear of the Lord" in the heart (Jer 32:40), being given a "new heart and a new spirit" (Ezek 36:26), being given a "heart of flesh" in exchange for the removal of a "heart of stone" (Ezek 36:26), and the idea of spiritual resurrection and "coming to life" (Ezek 37:1–14).

We have seen some of the terms used to describe the necessary transformation already in our discussion of the purpose of the Torah. These expressions seem naturally suited to appeal to the common man's sense of analogy, which helps him appreciate the radical and far-reaching effect that happens to the soul of the redeemed person that can only be accomplished by the supernatural power of God. These various metaphors and expressions, however, can be justifiably distilled to a somewhat deeper perspective.

Reason, man's ability to consider things soundly, is not the attribute that is directly affected by God's supernatural power. Sinful man's reasoning ability alone will never persuade him to respond favorably to the things of God. Indeed, his reason may even perceive the soundness of the claims of God revealed in scripture; but this alone will not urge him to respond favorably to the things of God, while he is yet unchanged. Neither is his *will* the attribute that is directly affected by the power of God. However clearly he may apprehend the correctness to take seriously the demands of God, man's will cannot be induced while he is yet unchanged.

These assessments are true because of the nature of these two attributes themselves. The reasoning ability is like the eye that sees a matter more or less clearly and truthfully insofar as it sees it formally—how something objectively manifests in the world, whether spiritually or materially. But this can be distinguished from how one reacts to something. I may see an approaching danger, and this may be perfectly true, but this rational perception alone will not mechanically cause my proper reaction of self-preservation. Regarding the will, I must also *desire* to preserve myself; I must want to avoid the coming danger. So then, there is always and necessarily something else that underlies willingness; there is yet a further distinguishable attribute of human nature that actually influences the will.

At the very core of all human behavior, and underlying one's rational volition, whether consciously or subconsciously, is the fact of *affection* that influences the will. It is the mysterious attribute of the emotional disposition, the "feelings," or the "taste" of the soul that is the basic ground or final reference for any decision that a person has to make. The simple concept of the "likes" and "dislikes" of a person's heart is *the critical human attribute* that has profound influence upon, and thorough control over, the entire behavior of any person. Even in the situations where we are faced with undesirable choices, we still ultimately decide, according to the appeal of our emotional disposition and the moral disposition at the very core, for the most desirable of distasteful courses of action for certain results. The affections are clearly at the root of the problem, as the prophet evinces when he urges *hatred* and *love* for the appropriate objects, saying, "Hate evil and love good!" שִׂנְאוּ־רָע וְאֶהֱבוּ טוֹב (Amos 5:15).

Now, this core attribute of the emotional disposition—the affections—is not a part of the makeup of our personality that we have any real control over to either produce or change. We are not free to dispose of it as we are our reason and volition, our thinking and acting. Mankind is, in fact, born into this slavery of *dislike for God*. We have free will or free agency insofar as we may will to do some thing or other, but we do not have the power to produce the fundamental affection necessary to incline toward the things of God. We cannot freely will to turn to God or serve him when there is no drawing approbation within our spirits, but only repugnancy toward the things of God.

This attribute was somehow mutable and was corrupted since the disobedience of man in the Garden of Eden. The human race is now *universally infected* with this evil moral disposition of hatred for his Creator, due especially to the radical distaste for the ethical demands of God. Mankind is also *universally desensitized* to this reprehensible state by the concomitant effects of arrogant pride and self-deception. This is the root cause of the ensuing history of mankind's indifference and rebellion to God, and the violence and injustice that mankind does to one another, as well as the cause of false and fanciful religious convictions. Distaste for the moral character of God.

So then, according to the Torah, if mankind is enslaved to a hatred for God, and if this is the root problem for him, then it is here, in this part of man, that Yahweh must do a work to remedy the problem. There is only one thing that can be done. Yahweh must *implant a new principle of love for him*, in such a manner that this new moral disposition will effectively and sufficiently displace the evil disposition (Deut 30:6; Ps 51:10; Ps 119:32, 36; Jer 31:33; Jer 32:39–40; Ezek 36:25–27). It is a gift of pure divine kindness. A man never asks for it, and a redeemed man will never thank enough for it. It is the very door of eternal life, and the very beginning of experienced love from God.

As we can observe from the whole Tanakh and can learn more precisely from the New Testament scriptures, however, the evil disposition or sinful nature is not completely removed but is somehow displaced from being the central personality of a redeemed man. So profound is the change that is effected on the heart that the redeemed person's *real and most sincere longing and delight* are toward the things of God. It is his relaxed and stable tendency rather than toward evil and unrighteousness. It is his new emotional enslavement. He cannot help but desire, in some measure, to be godly. Given this new sensitivity and proclivity toward God because of the basis of a new heart, the Holy Spirit can then persuade, stimulate, and direct the godly man's behavior by secret impressions and influences upon his mind. This is the directing or leading of the Spirit; the grace of *spiritual strengthening*.

The very critical difference between the New Covenant that Jeremiah predicts and the old covenant under the Mosaic era is that with the call through Moses for Israel to be Yahweh's special people, there was only the mere command but not the power of the Spirit to become such a devoted people as Yahweh deserved. But with the call of the New Covenant, there is given the power of the Spirit of God to be the kind of believing and obedient person that Yahweh requires for his fellowship. This is the very intention of the New Covenant: to provide the grace that is needed to ensure the glory of God in forming a people that he is not ashamed of.

The New Covenant does not actually displace the divine call of the old covenant inaugurated through Moses, but it does provide the spiritual ability for men and women to love that body of law that was commanded the Hebrews through Moses. The Law of Moses remained the standard for righteousness and the correct cultic worship of Yahweh so long as the temple service was sustained providentially. But when God finally revealed the Messiah that would serve his redemptive purposes in bringing in an everlasting atonement through the sacrifice of himself (which will be discussed later), then the shape of the covenant changed, because the external forms of the temple sacrificial system and the Levitical priesthood had been fulfilled and rendered obsolete.

11

The New Covenant:
Everyone Called Will Be Devoted

THE NEW COVENANT IS outlined in Jeremiah's prophecy (Jer 31:31–34). There are four elements involved:

1. God will put his law within the heart of Israel and Judah;
2. Yahweh will in reality be their God and they his people;
3. All the members who are inducted by the Holy Spirit into this New Covenant will immediately know God personally;
4. God will no longer retain the account of their sins for judgment but will freely forgive all of the sins of their existence before him, and so these will always be accepted and loved by him.

The first three may be summarized as saying that everyone called by God will indeed be devoted just as he requires. The fourth emphasizes the judicial safety in which God's people may serve him with the peace of a divinely cleansed conscience, knowing that their occasional guilt will never be a barrier to God's love and acceptance for those who desire the friendship of God in truth. This last element is actually made possible, as we learn in detail by the prophet Isaiah, by the priestly self-offering of the righteous Servant of Yahweh, who died as a substitute for sinners and was accepted as an atoning sacrifice by God (Isa 53:4–12).

This miraculous grace is what constitutes the realization of the New Covenant in that it *divinely ensures* that every person called will have been transformed by this same grace, which in turn ensures that the believer will fear and love God with the whole heart, in order to keep the covenant resolutely (Isa 54:13; Jer 31:31–34; Jer 32:40). Every member of the New Covenant will be devoted. Let us be clear and unmistaken. No one who has not received the gift of the Spirit, in order to be changed, will ever be able to serve God in an acceptable and salvific manner. That person who is not transformed by the Spirit of God will never be right with him, despite whatever seemingly correct religious behavior he may exhibit.

It is not *mere* apprehension of scriptural revelation that induces spiritual faith; rather, it is the Spirit of God that *induces* right apprehension and saving responsiveness. For as God has forever said in the Torah of Moses and spoke his unalterable word through his prophets, he will "circumcise the heart," and he will "put his Spirit in a man," so as to transform him (Deut 30:6; see Ezek 36:27). If men are not graced with this grace, then God will "loathe them," and regard them as "erring in their heart," and consider them as those who "do not really know his ways" (Ps 95:10). This is the divine assessment through the psalmist written many generations since the era of the Torah events, and yet he is compelled to give warning about the same failure as the wilderness generation because the Torah has taught him this evil is still possible as a relevant concern within Israel while they are under the economy of the old Mosaic covenant.

This same lesson of the danger of the Jews relying on religious falsehood is stated by the prophets, that though they are the descendants of the Patriarchs and were drawn into the covenant of Abraham through Moses, yet they served God "not in truth nor in righteousness" (Isa 48:1–2; Ezek 33:23–33). No matter what apparent zeal and devotion and outward form of religion men may show toward their perceived idea of service to God, if it is not really produced by the Spirit of God, it will be found unacceptable at the judgment. The scriptures bear witness to this truth, and it is also the specific indictment of the prophet Jeremiah that the Jews have always been susceptible to deceive themselves, believing that if they maintain a form of the religion of Yahweh by keeping its laws and institutions and yet do not have the fear and love that is only produced by the Spirit, they will be proven shamefully wrong in their claim to belong to God (Jer 7:1–15). It is in strict accordance with the condemnation of God that Jesus condemns the Jewish religious falsehood so prevalent in the Israelite culture of his day (Matt 23:1–36).

We must clearly understand what the *newness* of the New Covenant is and what remains the same; what things constitute a contrast and what things remain a continuum. If we trace the progress of divine revelation, we see that very early on, when God had established his covenant of grace with Abraham, he had learned also that by his believing and adhering to God's word and person that he was graciously accounted righteous before

God, or freely declared justified. It is after this spiritual fact that the Mosaic covenant was introduced, as the Hebrews were commanded to be his people and live according to this law. Then the majority failed to uphold that covenant, but we have seen that there was a relative few who were found to be right with God and truly loved and belonged to him. This faultiness of the first Mosaic covenant is what Yahweh has determined to do away with as he brings in the New Covenant.

The faultiness was specifically in the *ineffectiveness* of the mere external spoken and written word—the letter of the law—even though it had been God's spoken words to them. As long as the conscience alone was appealed to (while the heart remained unchanged), the lovingkindness and warnings would not have its impact on their personality as it ought to. This fault of the weakness of the external call to be God's special people is what God had decided to do away with. He had determined to realize or apply the new covenant of grace, with those whom he would yet call, with supernatural power providing the appropriate character in a man necessary to keep his covenant with sincere love and persistence.

So then, what remains the same is the way a man is justified before God, through faith and not through personal righteous effort; but what is different is the *actual participation* of the members of the covenanted body, by the Spirit infallibly placing *only those men who are transformed by grace* into this covenant. Salvation is the same, but the soul of the called is different. A relative few had been saved under the old covenant, but everyone called by the Spirit of God under the new covenant will be saved. The holiness of the covenant is the same, but the heart of every one of the renewed ones will truly love and pursue it.

To put it another way, the real newness of the New Covenant is both in the *extent* of the reality of sincere covenant-keeping devotion that will take place, and it is in the *manner* of the devotion that will be found within this relationship—because every one called by God will have been provided with a new heart to keep the covenant, as opposed to being "taken by the hand" according to the nature of the external call. It is that *everyone* כולם of those persons, who are effectively called out of the world through the change by God's Spirit, will certainly make up the true congregation of Israel and no other (Jer 31:31–34). It will not be as the recorded phenomena of the old covenant, where one here and there has been found to have real saving faith and love toward God, such as an Abraham, a Moses, a David, etc., or other small scattered portion of the general populace of Israel.

12

The Servant of Yahweh:
The New Mediator of the New Covenant

THE TORAH EMBODIES THE beginning revelations from God. And, as we have seen, within this body of initial disclosures of the redemptive purposes of God are embedded foundational declarations by which the mind and will of God may be known regarding mankind's spiritual salvation. These declarations are also our surest principles for interpreting the scriptures so as to correctly understand the works of God within human history.

According to the Torah, one of these foundational disclosures is that God wills to generally speak his mind and will to his people through the agency (or mediation) of the Hebrew prophets (Deut 18:15–19), as is the reverent observation of these prophets themselves (Dan 9:6, 10). He wills to use these servants in the disclosure of himself and his determined purposes to his called people. The prophet Amos declared, "Surely the Lord God does nothing unless he reveals his secret counsel to his servants the prophets." יהוה דבר כי אם־גלה סודו אל־עבדיו הנביאים כי לא יעשה אדני (Amos 3:7). God rarely spoke directly to man, such as when he spoke directly to the Patriarchs and Moses. So then, there can be observed a continual stream, however intermittent, of divinely ordained spokesmen revealing yet more and more information concerning the redemptive purposes of God in relation to his called people.

This progressive revelation can be summarized as follows: After the giving of the Covenant of Grace with Abraham and his descendants, God raised up Moses for the deliverance of theses descendants from Egyptian slavery, the establishment of the national covenant with the Israelites, and the giving of covenantal law. Then God declared through Moses, his eminent servant, that he will yet raise up succeeding prophets who will further be employed to reveal the mind and will of God to the Hebrews.

Moses clearly implies that God had not finished speaking his mind and will to the people when God had employed him; but that there will be yet another like him. Let no one say that only Moses must be revered and no other alongside him! And God is clear in the book of Isaiah that the one who obeys his servant is the one who trusts him (Isa 50:10). And, negatively, Daniel is clear in his indictment of "all Israel" that they did not listen to "the Lord's servants the prophets" (Dan 9:5–12). According to the Hebrews' history, there were first the Judges and then special prophets beginning with Samuel. Then there were the later prophets who wrote much of the body of Hebrew scripture, such as the books of Isaiah, Jeremiah, and Ezekiel.

All of these men that God, in his wisdom and providence, raised up were to be revered as though God himself were speaking to the people directly (Deut 18:18–19; see also Exod 23:20–23). They were divinely appointed mediators. They were to be heeded and obeyed if the people wished to continue as the beloved of God. This is the holy conviction of the Hebrew prophets themselves who spoke for the Holy One (Jer 15:19; Jer 20:9). It is also extremely important to understand that some of these holy prophets who spoke for God began to progressively reveal that there was to be *a particularly chosen servant* who will effectively accomplish what is necessary for a realized and permanent salvation to take place.

It is not within the scope of this book to explore deeply what the prophets have disclosed through the scriptures concerning this specially chosen Servant of Yahweh, but only to touch upon the fact that this is a significant revelation found in the Hebrew Bible and should be observed with all fear and trembling, as God would have it to be (Isa 66:2). There are very important things said about this one particular Servant that God will raise up, much of which is found in the book of Isaiah within the "songs of the Servant of Yahweh" portions (Isa 42:1–9; Isa 49:1–7; Isa 50:4–9; Isa 52:13—53:12; Isa 61:1–3). And it is in conjunction with the revelation of this special Servant that God asserts that, though former things have come to pass, he is now declaring new things that will spring forth (Isa 42:9). Such things as:

He is chosen by God, and so is not to be despised by the Israelites (Isa 42:1; Isa 49:1–3; Isa 50:10). He will be completely innocent and righteous, and will bring forth righteousness to the nations; and so the sinful nation of Israel is not intended here as this servant, nor any of the other prophets who typically confess their sinfulness (Isa 42:1, 4; Isa 53:5–12). He will be a "covenant" for the people of Israel, as well as a "light" to the gentiles (Isa 42:6; Isa 49:5–6). He will be despised and rejected by the people of Israel and be considered cursed by God as a sinner, rather than be revered as one of the former prophets (Isa 49:7; Isa 50:6; Isa 52:14; Isa 53:3, 9, 12). He will suffer oppression and death at the hands of the people (Isa 50:6; Isa 52:14; Isa 53:7–12). He will die for the sins of other people, by the will of God (Isa 53:4–6, 8, 10–12). He will make his appearance and be killed before the destruction of the second temple (Mal 3:1; Dan 9:25–26). He will be resurrected from the grave and enjoy the results of his commission (Isa 53:10–11). He will effect atonement and justification (Isa 53:7–8, 10–12; see Dan 9:24). He will effect spiritual deliverance from the bondage of the sinful nature (Isa 42:7; Isa 49:9; Isa 61:1). He will fulfill the typology of the earthly temple service and displace the priestly sacrificial service (Isa 53:7, 10; see Dan 9:24). He will be the human embodiment of Yahweh himself, as surely as God had appeared in the form of a man in the record of the Torah (Gen 3:8; Gen 18:1–2; Gen 28:13; Gen 32:24–30; Isa 9:6–7; Mic 5:4).

With the inspired Jewish writings of the New Covenant era (the New Testament), we are given to know who this Servant of Yahweh is, and we are told who the prophesied Messiah is (Acts 2:22–36; Acts 3:18–26; Acts 7:51–53; Acts 26:13–15, 22–23; Rom 1:1–4; 1 Pet 1:10–12). His name is Yeshua (Jesus). It is he whom we must listen to and obey. It is he who has died for the sake of sinners that they might be reconciled to God and justified in his sight. It is he who is the mediator of God because he is given as a "covenant" for the people. It is he whom we must turn to for atonement because he is the Righteous One that died for the guilt of many, according to the design of God.

Let no Jewish person (or gentile) say that he does not need a mediator for salvation, because God has forever disclosed through his prophets that he has provided one, who has suffered a vicarious death for sinful Israel. Nor let them say that the Messiah is yet to come, since he had suddenly come to his temple, but was despised and suffered as the Servant was predicted to be, before the destruction of that very temple (Dan 9:24–26; Mal 3:1–4). He is the substantive fulfillment of the provisional mediation typified in the Levitical priesthood and the curtain of the Holy of Holies in the temple, practiced since the inauguration of the Mosaic institutions of the old desert faith. If this be the holy determination of God, who will be so arrogant as to reject it?!

When Jeremiah predicted the giving of the New Covenant, the time of its inauguration was left open, stating merely "days are coming" (Jer 31:31). The fact is, however, that according to the scriptures, none of the prophets or servants who God has raised up for his purposes were ever announced with an arrival time and with a name to be known by. But the Servant of Yahweh was special in that he was foretold in such a manner. Still, it is with the Servant of Yahweh as with the other prophets when it came to his actual appearance. God was pleased to reveal him in his own good timing and not before. But, as we learn from the prophet Isaiah, as surely as the surprising call and "anointing" of the pagan Cyrus to fulfill God's purposes of providing deliverance and restoration of the people of Judah and Jerusalem was disbelieved by them (Isa 44:24—45:13), so also the commission and inauguration of "new things" by the Servant of Yah- weh will be disbelieved (Isa 42:9; Isa 49:7; Isa 52:13—53:3). Nevertheless, God will prevail over his disbelieving enemies among his people with the zeal of a warrior (Isa 42:10–13; Isa 49:7). This Servant of Yahweh, Jesus, inaugurates the New Covenant because he is given as a "covenant" to the people (Isa 42:6). In him the covenant is *really fulfilled,* and being con- nected to him is to be in covenant with Yahweh.

It must be fully grasped by every Jew (and every gentile) who wishes to be lovingly known by God that he has forever declared through his prophets that the original national covenant given through Moses would be eventually superseded and displaced with the new national covenant— the spiritual one that is completely effected by the Spirit of God (Jer 31:31–32); not the foundational Covenant of Grace given to Abraham and the Hebrews in him, but the subsequent Sinai compact made with the descendants of Abraham, the people of Israel. This covenant, which generally effected the exposure of sin and its condemnation, will be re- placed with the new one, which comes with the supernatural assistance of the Spirit of God resulting in the glorious worship and service of the living God.

It must also be seriously understood, however, that for the religious Jew who, in the divine prerogative, happens to be left to the sway of his own sinful nature and is not influenced by the Spirit of God for his ev- erlasting good will naturally *default* to an unbiblical recourse of life. This recourse will always consist of trusting in the unspiritual idea of keeping the practice of laws and commandments and notions of earthly goodness for the meriting of favor and justification of life before God. He will be left to adopt, due to his inescapable conscience and the deceitfulness of his own heart, a life of slavery to the letter of the law, trying to measure up his personal behavior to a mere formal description of the will of God. But he will never have a spiritual, profound, and helpless delight in either the deeper purpose or the performance of these laws, which is to reflect the glorious character of God.

But for the Jew (and the gentile) who is renewed by the Spirit of God, his heart has an unspoken and helpless reliance on the mercy of God for his ultimate acceptance before him, resulting in a free and gracious justification of life and the forgiveness of sins. There is not an ultimate dependence upon performance of laws (whether of the letter or the conscience) because he knows there is no perfect keeping of them, and so a holy God could never justify his existence. So, the renewed man is begotten with a *freedom from defaulting* to slavery to keep the law perfectly for meriting justification, while the unchanged man proceeds with his existence already prone to self-reliance. These two different courses of life, especially for the Jew, are what is meant by the allegory of the "Earthly Jerusalem" with her "children born into slavery," and the "Heavenly Jerusalem" with her "freeborn children," spoken by the Apostle Paul in his letter to the Galatian churches (Gal 4:21–31).

13

The New Spiritual Temple

IT IS THE CONSIDERED opinion of this author that, since there is a new covenant given that consists of a *perfect priestly sacrifice for sin offered once for all,* then there is also no need for a continued Levitical priestly service or its material temple. It must be honestly acknowledged that both the historical Jerusalem temples and the Levitical priestly service had been sovereignly destroyed and interrupted due to divine punishment for Israel's disobedience to the covenant, not the least of which consisted of not believing the message of, and obeying, the Servant of Yahweh who provided a vicarious atonement with his life.

According to, and consistent with, our study of the message of the Torah, there was to be further prophetism beyond the ministry of Moses. The very last of the prophets raised up by God for the purpose of revealing his closing redemptive acts among men are, first of all, Jesus the Messiah, and also his appointed Apostles and their contemporary prophets; that is, those who saw and believed on the Lord Jesus and were anointed by the Spirit of God to bear witness to his mission (Matt 28:16–20; Luke 24:44–49; Acts 1:1–3, 8; Acts 10:34–43; 1 Cor 12:28; Eph 2:20; Eph 4:7–12; Heb 1:1–2; Heb 2:1–4).

Consequent to the inauguration of the New Covenant, it was certainly the prediction of the supreme prophet Jesus the Messiah (See Acts 3:18–23) that God would have the second temple destroyed for Israel's rejection of Yahweh's Servant, just as he had the first temple destroyed along with Jerusalem (Ezra 5:11–12; Jer 16:9–13; Jer 22:5–9; Jer 25:8–11; Jer 26:18; Zech 7:11–14; Matt 23:37–38; Matt 24:2; Mark 13:2; Luke 19:41–44). More importantly, with the New Covenant came *the new manner of God's dwelling* among his sanctified and devoted people (whether Jew or gentile), that of his abiding presence within the heart, and within the midst, of those who have been changed by his grace. God had adumbrated this "new thing" of dwelling intimately with the reverent person (Isa 57:15), and lovingly looking upon him who feared him with the only approval that mattered in the world, when he expressly disdains the material temple as being too inadequate (Isa 66:1–2).

This view is confirmed by the teaching of the Lord Jesus and the inspired understanding of the Apostles in the New Testament writings. Jesus declared that he himself would raise up a "sanctuary" ναος in the place of the destroyed temple with the resurrection of his own body. And this proves to be the true dwelling of God, in the collective body of redeemed believers in the Messiah Jesus as "a holy sanctuary in the Lord" ναον αγιον εν Κυριω (John 2:19–21; 1 Cor 3:16–17; 1 Cor 6:19; 2 Cor 6:16; Eph 2:20–22; Rev 21:1–5, 22). And the Apostle John writes that he was blessed to see the New Jerusalem, "having the glory of God," "coming down out of heaven" (Rev 21:1–27). He specifically states that there is no sanctuary in it because the Almighty God and the Lamb are its sanctuary (Rev 21:22).

The supporting reasons, that there will not be a third material temple built by divine mandate but there will only be a spiritual temple among the spiritually redeemed ones, are:

The Perfect and Eternal Atonement. The New Covenant is founded upon the perfect and eternal priesthood and sacrifice of the Servant of Yahweh who fulfilled, for all time, the types and shadows of the Levitical service of the earthly cult employed under the old Mosaic covenant, and who *completely satisfied* both the penal requirements of the law and its demands for righteousness (Isa 53:4–12; John 1:29; 1 Pet 2:24–25). There is now, with the establishment of the better covenant, no need for yet another material temple with Levitical priests and animal sacrifices (Heb 10:1–18). And even though God promises, in "days coming," that the Levitical priests "shall never lack a man to offer burnt offerings, etc." (Jer 33:17–18), we know from another prophet that God has raised up another Priest "after the order of Melchizedek" (Ps 110:4; see Heb 7:11–28), rather than the order of Aaron, to be his perfect eternal Mediator, and a "Lord" who rules the people of God (Ps 110:1–3; Isa 9:6–7; Jer 23:5–6; Jer 33:14–16; Zech 3:8–10; Zech 6:12–13). And so, in this one Servant will be "a priest on his throne" (Zech 6:13). He will indeed both replace the Levitical order and fulfill the everlasting provision of a "Levitical" priest to minister to Yahweh.

The Symbolic Temple Descriptions. The exilic description of the dimensions and arrangements of the temple and its environs, seen in the visions of the restoration by Ezekiel, are somewhat different than the Mosaic descriptions; and such a temple envisaged was indeed never built during the reconstruction of Jerusalem and her second temple. Certain aspects of Ezekiel's temple construction are, in fact, physically impossible to realize, and so cannot be a material temple description—such things as the water flowing from under the threshold of the temple flowing east and increasing in depth unto the Dead Sea and even desalinating it and giving life to creatures, with trees growing along its banks that are always blooming and giving fruit that not only feeds but heals (Ezek 47:1–12; Zech 14:8; Rev 21:1–27; Rev 22:1–2). Also the tribal geographical allotments are remarkably different than the original Mosaic directives in the Torah (Ezek 48:1–29). Supporting these symbolic characteristics is the poetic imagery of Jerusalem herself in her glorious restoration, with the use of precious gems to depict the spiritual value of the future city of Jerusalem along with her redeemed citizens (Isa 54:11–13). These facts surely reveal the symbolic nature of this temple description.

The Messiah Will Build His Temple. The former temples were built according to the divine directives spoken through the prophets, but here this is conspicuously absent, and there is no more prophetism since the destruction of the second temple (70 CE), which would give the divine mandate to build yet another temple. It is very telling that, during the post-exilic construction of the second temple, the rebuilding project was especially exhorted by the prophets Haggai and Zechariah (Ezra 5:1–2), yet neither they nor the leadership of the community consulted the Ezekiel description of the temple, but rather referred to the established descriptions of Moses found in the Torah (Ezra 3:2, 4; Ezra 6:14, 18). And yet Zechariah must have perceived that this material temple that was being rebuilt was not to be the ultimate temple, nor that the Levitical priesthood was to be the ideal mediation, because he predicts that Yahweh's Servant, "the Branch," will "build the temple of the Lord" and will be "a priest on his throne" (Zech 6:12–13).

So, during the very building of the second temple by the Israelite community, Zechariah declares that *the promised Servant will build Yahweh's true temple.* This was long before the historical destruction of that second temple then being built, and yet another temple was still necessary to be built for God. Therefore, let no Jew assert that the Messiah has not come because a supposed third material temple will be built; for Zechariah understood this insight to mean a special temple beside the material temple then being built! Moreover, there were no predictions of the prolonged judgment period (now 2,000 years), nor any specific prediction of its end, as there was with the first temple. And there is not to be a prophet raised up for the matter because there is no more prophetism, because God has finally spoken through the Son whom he sent and those who heard him (Heb 1:1–2; Heb 2:3).

Yahweh's dwelling is the holy people. The prophet Ezekiel records the significant revelation that Yahweh will have his new eternal dwelling, his sanctuary, located *within the sanctified lives* of those who reciprocate his love and enjoy his lordship over them (Ezek 37:24–28; Ezek 39:25–29). God will restore a sanctified Israel to the land that he had originally given to them through covenant promise, and also he will dwell within those who, being transformed by his Spirit, will have him as their God and who will be his people—even as it was essentially expressed concerning the original covenant with Abraham (Gen 17:7–8). The prophecies in Ezekiel concerning the restoration of Israel to her land with the complete devotion of all the house of Israel are more likely the descriptions of the eschatological consummation to be found in the age to come, though even now during the messianic age inaugurated with the coming of the Messiah Jesus, they have their partial and gradual fulfillment.

The amazing establishment of the State of Israel in 1948 seems to be the precursor to the blessed age yet to come; however, it is certain that the miraculous resurrection of the "dry bones" of Israel into the revived nation of God and the restoration to the land (Ezek 37:1–14) had not occurred with post-exilic Judea, nor in the establishment of the modern Jewish state. Rather, the beginning of the blessedness of the Spirit's renewal did occur with the coming of the Messiah Jesus—the righteous Branch, the second David, the good shepherd-king of Israel—being manifested in those individual redeemed ones who were granted eternal life (Matt 26:28; Mark 14:24; Luke 22:20; John 10:27–28; John 17:1–3).

When these eschatological determinations that God has planned for his called people of Israel are revealed through the prophet (Ezek 37:25–28), he first mentions that he will finally place his sanctuary "among," or, "in their midst" בתוכם forever (v 26). This is explained further with a definite spiritual sense of "sanctuary" and not a material temple. The language found in this Ezekiel passage makes this point more clearly:

"My dwelling will be over them," or, "upon them" וְהָיָה מִשְׁכָּנִי עֲלֵיהֶם (not among them, as a mere building), which entails his "being their God and they being his people" (v 27). There would be, therefore, no need for another material temple because *Yahweh's people will be the temple*. This understanding is expressed in the apostolic writings of the New Testament (1 Cor 6:19; 2 Cor 6:16; Eph 2:19–22; Rev 7:15).

Ezekiel also records the significant declaration of the divine axiom that the world would know that Yahweh truly sanctifies and enjoys his people whenever he has the symbol of his dwelling in the midst of the people of Israel forever—his "sanctuary" among them (v 28). This "sanctuary" is not a material temple but will be a spiritual temple comprised of those in whom God dwells by his Spirit, having been built by the Messiah, the Second David, through his reigning in the hearts and lives of his purified and separated ones (Zech 6:12–13; Rev 21:1–27). This will be the manifest divine presence in the midst of his people. And God had already intimated earlier through his prophet Isaiah that the truly desirable and more meaningful dwelling place is within the hearts and lives of the ones who fear him (Isa 57:15; Isa 66:1–2). Yahweh declares that the nations will certainly appreciate and "know" that he effectually "sanctifies" his people to be the holy and righteous nation that was intended by God all along when he is seen to be indwelling them by his Spirit (v 28).

Consequently, there will be no material temple in Israel while God is not loved and obeyed according to the revelation of his servants the prophets, and while his sent one the Messiah Jesus is continually despised. And so, it would seem that the current general state of affairs of the Jews would continue on until, as we know from the prophet Paul, the "fullness" of the gentiles come into salvation and the Kingdom of God, and then "all Israel will be saved" (Rom 11:25–27).

14

The Restored Davidic Kingdom

THE FURTHER PROPHETISM ANNOUNCES that there will be a *restored* Davidic kingdom with another "David" ruling over the people of God. In the foundational revelation of the Torah, Jacob prophesied that it would be the tribe of Judah that shall always have the *honor of providing the divinely ordained ruler* for the people of Israel; that "the scepter shall not depart from Judah, nor the ruler's staff from between his feet" (Gen 49:10; Ps 78:67–68). Later in Israel's history, after the period of the Judges, and the twelve tribes having had their first king in the installment of Saul (who had failed in his office due to disobedience to God's directives), the prophet Samuel is commissioned to anoint David the son of Jesse as the divinely elected king of Israel, which fulfills Jacob's prophecy concerning the tribe of Judah (1 Sam 16:1–13).

David was a godly man filled with the Spirit of God since his anointing as the king of Israel, who was described as "a man after God's own heart" (1 Sam 13:14). Though he was not sinless and indeed sinned shamefully at times, still, by the grace of God he *typified* the ideal king of Israel. His was generally a rule of righteousness and faithfulness to the Mosaic covenant (1 Kgs 2:1–3), exercising a godly reign over the whole house of Israel within an extensive kingdom (Ps 78:70–72). Moreover, despite the imperfection of David's reign, God in his sovereign lovingkindness determined to establish his house and his dynasty as the royal line over the Kingdom of Israel forever (2 Sam 7:8–17; Ps 89:19–37).

But because the general nation of Israel, both before and after David's generation, has failed to be the pious people of Yahweh according to the faith and righteousness stipulated in the Mosaic covenant, God has determined to bring about this glorious kingdom with the establishment of a *purely spiritual kingdom,* formed by the grace of the New Covenant and the installment of Jesus, his elected king in spiritual Zion—his specially loved "son," "the righteous branch of Jesse" (Ps 2:6–9; Isa 9:6–7; Isa 11:1–10; Isa 16:5; Isa 35:1–10; Jer 23:5–6; Jer 33:14–16; Ezek 37:15–28; Amos 9:11–15; Mic 4:1–8; Zech 3:8–10; Matt 5:17–18).

God had expressed his desire that the nation of Israel, formed by his kindness through the leadership of Moses and Aaron, would be a holy people full of reverence, love, faith, and gratitude, with persistent devotion (Exod 19:5, 9; Num 14:11; Deut 6:1–9; Deut 7:6; Deut 26:16–19; Deut 28:9–10). And even though they failed him, God solemnly resolved that he would yet be glorified throughout the whole earth eventually, through his sovereign working and purposes in salvation history, despite all apparent setbacks within human history (Num 14:21).

The specific characteristic of the new Davidic kingdom is in its nature as a purely spiritual kingdom, during the present evil age, in which all the redeemed individuals, wherever they are found, will be *sweetly ruled in their lives* through the effective influence of their renewed hearts being knit to the Lord Jesus in genuine love, obedience, and dying loyalty. Because they have been implanted with faith and love for the Messiah Jesus, the second David, they will naturally live according to his lordship. This grace ensures the *reality and stability* of the restored Davidic kingdom, which could not be accomplished by the mere appeal to the conscience of ancient Israel. Moreover, because the Lord Jesus, the son of David, has risen from the dead and lives forevermore, he thus fulfills God's promise to David that the throne of his kingdom would *be established forever* (2 Sam 7:13, 16; see Matt 21:4–5, 9; Acts 2:32–33; Heb 1:3). In the latter days, God will cause by his Spirit the *national resurrection and reunion* of Israel and Judah, and these transformed lovers of the Messiah Jesus will have him as their one king, God's servant "David" (Ezek 37:11–14, 24–25).

The prophets have revealed that God wills to effect this glorious kingdom of godly and devoted people through the great program of the New Covenant, which was inaugurated by the coming and work of the Servant of Yahweh, Jesus. In this one holy Servant is combined several glorious roles:

1. The office of prophet who accomplishes God's will by the communications of his mouth (Isa 49:2);

2. The office of priest who accomplishes perfect everlasting atonement for his people (Isa 53:10–12; Dan 9:24);

3. The office of king who rules with perfect righteousness and judgment in his reign, and has perfect sway over the hearts of those belonging to his kingdom (Isa 9:6–7; Isa 11:1–5; Jer 23:5–6; Jer 33:15–16; Ezek 37:24–28).

15

The New Revelation of Yahweh: God With Us

BOTH THE TORAH AND the prophets have revealed the very principle by which these roles of prophet, priest, and king can be understood as combined and fulfilled in one person, and be fulfilled perfectly with the characteristic of righteousness. It is the tremendous event of *God taking the form of a son of man* for the purpose of demonstrating his grace to completely love, help, identify with, and commune with the people whom he has determined to redeem. The exclusive love that God is pleased to give to his elect ones consists of the giving of himself to be enjoyed in a personal and intimate fellowship. In order to more fully realize this closeness, identity, and unity of feeling, and to approximate the warmth and significance of the family or of marriage, God joined himself to human nature to become one of us, to love and be loved as can only be experienced within the relationships of humanity. He appeared as a man of flesh and blood, with a feeling and thinking soul that can realistically relate to us as fellow creatures.

The scriptures basically reveal this amazing and critical fact in two ways:

1. The Hebrew Scriptures have accounts that *adumbrate divine incarnation,* by either the actual appearances, or the future intimations, of God taking the form of a man or an angelic being (Gen 3:8; Gen 18:1–33; Gen 32:24–30; Exod 23:20–23; Josh 5:13—6:5; Judg 6:11–24; Isa 7:14; Isa 9:6–7; Zech 9:9–10; Zech 12:8; Mal 3:1–3).

2. The New Testament Scriptures *certify, ex post facto,* the actual incarnation of God as a man (Matt 1:22–23; Matt 4:13–16; Matt 11:27; Matt 24:30–31; Matt 28:18; Mark 1:1–8; Mark 14:62; Luke 1:35; Luke 3:2–6, 16–17; John 1:1, 30; John 8:58; John 10:27–30, 38; John

14:7–11; John 16:15; John 17:5; John 18:6; John 20:28; Rom 9:5; 2 Cor 5:19; Phil 2:5–11; Col 1:15–19; Col 2:9; Titus 2:13; Heb 1:2–12; 1 John 5:20; Rev 2:8).

The Tanakh recounts, at times, the amazing and unashamed events of the appearing of Yahweh in the form and nature of a man to more intimately communicate to his servants. God willed to do these visitations purely from his sovereign and amazing kindness. He did not have to, but could have sustained a strictly remote correspondence with his people, or only used the agency of a mediator. It does not matter if these visitations of Yahweh that are recorded in the Torah were not actual incarnations at this early stage but were only made somehow to seem as real men in appearance and behavior. The fact remains that God does not regard himself as so different and removed from his creation that he is incapable or disdains to somehow enter into space and time and matter, as a man among men or as an angelic being interfacing with men, for the purposes of gracious intervention. These scripture accounts forcefully teach that God can and wills to condescend to the realm of humanity, not to abdicate his divinity and shamefully lower the order of his being (which is impossible and unthinkable), but to relate more meaningfully with mankind for the sake of his glorious lovingkindness.

The book of Daniel clearly discloses God's determination to *involve a chosen man* in his redemptive program and sovereign rule in the world. "One like a son of man" was brought with the clouds of heaven to Yahweh and received, essentially, God's divine glory (Dan 7:13–14; see Mark 8:38). This man came by God's commission ("with the clouds of heaven"), and was given the divine dominion, the divine glory, and the worship of all the nations of the world. The phrase "son of man" always means, to the ordinary Hebrew person, a fellow human being (See, for examples, Ezek 2:1, 3, 6, 8; Prov 8:31); and Daniel consistently uses the term denoting a frail, mortal, ordinary man אנש (Dan 3:10; Dan 5:5, 7; Dan 6:12; Dan 7:4). It was given to the Messiah Jesus and his Apostles to positively proclaim the fact of an actual and permanent incarnation of God as a man among men.

The Matthean gospel account records that the miraculous birth of Jesus fulfilled the typological prophecy (which had a double intention) concerning the reassuring sign that God had given to the distressed King Ahaz of Judah during the prophetic service of Isaiah. The sign seems to have been the *surprising and unexpected pregnancy* of a young lady (perhaps the prophet's wife) that would give birth to a son, who God determines would be called *Immanuel,* meaning "God with us" (Matt 1:18–23; see Isa 7:14). That sign, brought about by divine providence for Ahaz's benefit, was to reassure him that God was committed to the Davidic dynasty for its defense against foreign attack, if only the current king would be trusting and obedient to the Israelite covenant. But its deeper meaning was to announce, through a reoccurrence of a singular divine providence, the incarnation of God for the sake of David's kingdom, Israel.

Again, the apostolic proclamations are unashamed and rest securely on the plain accounts and prophecies of the Tanakh. God had somehow united himself to an especially chosen (and sinless) human being for the purpose of conveying the grace of redemption with the *closest possible contact and the fullest possible solidarity* with the ones to whom he gives his love and himself.

16

The Renewed World

THE PROPHETS ANNOUNCE THAT there will be new heavens (the visible skies) and a new earth, or, a renewed world, because they will be changed like a worn-out garment (Ps 102:25–26; Isa 65:17–25; Isa 66:22). They use very poetic descriptions to depict, in a forceful and yet understandable way, what is essentially strange or different to the inhabitants of earth as it is currently known. Familiar life scenes, which are yet amazingly different due to the better conditions of the glorious order of the divine renewal, are infused with the blessedness of peace and righteousness that can only come from the power of God.

It is difficult to determine the precise nature of this renewal of the world, but it is doubtless some kind of supernatural transformation that renders it more suited to be the everlasting residence of the redeemed people of God living directly in his presence (2 Pet 3:10–13). Isaiah himself often employs the language of metaphor, involving either the personified behavior of otherwise lifeless components, such as trees and mountains, or the transformed behavior of the animals, to emphasize a significant condition or event effected by the power of God in the course of redemptive history (See, for examples, Isa 2:2; Isa 11:6–9; Isa 35:1–10; Isa 36:6; Isa 37:27; Isa 41:17–20; Isa 55:12–13).

Since there was no divine moral concern about the behavior of such animals as lions and snakes, the subdued nature of the ferocious animal kingdom is not the point. It is that there will be *no more sinful harm* between man and man, which can be pictured by the conquering and destructive behavior of these animals. The peace of the renewed world will be thoroughgoing in that both the remaining sinful nature of redeemed individuals and consequently the exposure to evil mistreatment from others will be completely removed. This is the really important thing.

This new creation of the sinless age to come will be such that God himself will rejoice and be glad in both his people and Jerusalem, and he invites his redeemed ones to do so also (Isa 65:18–19). Jerusalem is the focal point of this divine concern as the holy mountain that is raised up, in a spiritual sense, over all the mountains of the world. Zion's righteous laws will pervade, as waters cover the sea, the hearts and minds of all the nations, who will be drawn to her. Because of this perfect inward love for God's will, there will be no evil or harm done in all the earth. It is the age when all the wicked and all sin will have been purged from the world, and it has been prepared or changed for the eternal home of the redeemed people of God (Isa 35:8; Isa 52:1; Isa 65:25; Rev 21:27).

This glorious age to come will be completely inaugurated by the fulfilled reign of the righteous Branch of Jesse, the righteous Anointed One (Isa 11:1–10). He is the second "David," who will be Prince among God's people, along with the amazing conditions of a renewed earth (Ezek 34:23–30). But in the meantime, during this present evil age, there is certainly a sense that this glorious dominion is already being realized and fulfilled in a spiritual way with the reigning of the Messiah Jesus in the hearts and lives of those who have received him as their Lord and Savior. Spiritually, this reign of the Messiah is already real in the hearts of his disciples, where there is the dominating kingdom of "righteousness and peace and joy in the Holy Spirit" (Rom 14:17). And so, metaphorically speaking, the dangers and wild beasts of *unloving behavior* among godly men have been definitively removed. But then, in the kingdom of the age to come, there will be the perfection of this harmless existence extending throughout the whole world when only the redeemed ones will remain present with the intimate presence of their holy Lord.

17

Israel and the Land

THE HEBREW PROPHETS REVEAL a succession of significant events that are predetermined as the divine purposes for the people of Israel and the land that was given to them, which will lead up to the bright and glorious future of "the last days." This last comprehensive epoch of redemptive history will progress to, and culminate in, the eternal age to come. It must always be remembered that these concerns are anchored in the critical divine initiative of the election and call of Abraham to serve God and to relocate to the land of Canaan. This spiritual calling and the granting of the physical land are permanently bound together in the mind of God and forever registered in the Torah.

Israel will never perish from the earth as a people loved and honored with the call of Yahweh, and they will remain as surely as the ordinances of the sun and moon will remain forever even into the age to come (Jer 31:35–37). Despite the persistent historical failure of Israel to be a glorious and holy covenanted nation unto Yahweh, there are many prophecies which reveal the determination of God to finally restore both his honor and their real redemption.

Abraham was selected out of humanity to begin a radical life-service of worshiping God (El Shaddai) exclusively and to depart from his Mesopotamian idolatry and homeland. He was commanded to remove himself to the land of Canaan, which would be given to him and his descendants forever. He was assured that he would be blessed, that his descendants would be greatly multiplied, and that through him all the nations would eventually be blessed (Gen 12:1–3; Gen 15:5; Gen 17:1–8; Gen 22:17–18).

It is clear to sound reasoning and by the emphasis of the words of God that the essence of the blessing is to have El Shaddai, this God, as one's own loving god and to belong to him in turn (Gen 17:7–8). But also, the people of God are destined to have a place on earth to live, and so a particular land is promised to Abraham and his descendants. As surely as God sovereignly chooses a portion of humanity to be his people, so he also chooses a portion of the earth to be for his people (Gen 13:14–17; Gen 17:8). Even though the land of Canaan was inhabited by various heathen nations prior to the arrival and conquest of Israel, God determined to displace them, doubtless for their sinful demerit before him, who owed them no protection or rights.

Sometime after Israel was settled in the land of Canaan, God (by now known as Yahweh) disclosed that Jerusalem, situated on the small hill called Mount Zion, would be the place for his special, localized presence, which was represented by the phrase, "My name shall be there" (Deut 12:11; 1 Kgs 8:29; 1 Kgs 11:13; Ps 78:68–69). It was not his true dwelling, which was Heaven (1 Kgs 8:27, 30; Isa 66:1), but was a representative type of the real heavenly dwelling manifesting his special presence among men. It served as a spiritual center through which he would accomplish the redemption of his people and through which he would be approached and worshiped in the Israelite cult (Deut 12:5, 11; Deut 15:20; Deut 16:2; Deut 17:8; Deut 18:6).

One of the reasons that God chose Mount Zion to house his sanctuary (the temple) is because to men, a mountain is a solid, safe, and immovable place. This security in turn is fit to be a representative type of the sure and unshakable foundation of God's redemptive program. That is, whenever a man turns to God for salvation in whatever location in the world he happens to be, God will respond to him through the atoning service that is accomplished and the priestly mediation that he has established in Jerusalem. These salvific provisions were intentionally centered in this particular location on earth through providential historical events that were ultimately types of the real and better atonement and mediation accomplished through the Messiah Jesus, which also were accomplished in Jerusalem. This place of his sanctuary will be the spiritual safe haven for those who seek and trust him for salvation (Ps 43:3–4; Ps 53:6; Ps 78:68–69).

After God had established the national Mosaic covenant with Israel, the people had generally failed to keep it and were formally condemned in accordance with the covenant stipulations (Deut 27:15–26; Deut 28:15–68; Deut 32:1–25). Nevertheless, the foundational covenant with Abraham and his descendants is always being kept as the sure unilateral purpose of God (Exod 32:11–14; Ezek 37:25; Mic 7:18–20). But it was the sinners of his people, however many they be, who would be punished for breaking the covenant (Exod 32:33; Amos 9:10). In keeping with this unshakeable purpose of God for his people and the land he gave them, he has prophesied his holy determination to vindicate himself of this disgrace. He will ultimately avenge his oppressed people and atone for both the land and the people וכפר אדמתו עמו, because these concerns directly affect his honor as he willed to glorify his name by purposing a holy people situated in a holy land in the fallen world (Deut 32:34–43).

The manner through which God will clear his name of apparent shame is by the exertion of his sovereign power in causing a preserved remnant of fallen Israel to be created as his true servants, with sincere faith and love, along with restoring them to live in the land he gave them, never to be displaced again (Exod 32:12; Deut 32:26–27; Ezek 36:16–24). But God will do even greater things than these, as though this was too little. He will cause the gentile nations, who have been the instruments of his chastisement toward Israel, to receive the light of his salvation also. They will be caused to turn to him and will honor his chosen people as the ones who first knew the true God (Isa 49:5–7, 22–23).

Because of the divine judgment for Israel's failure in the national covenant, she began to experience foreign oppression and eventually exile and dispersion. The people, as the sinful portion, would be rejected and abandoned (Jer 6:30; Jer 7:29), while the land itself was ruined and neglected repeatedly. This apparent abandonment was to continue until the birth of the prophesied ruler who will reign in the majesty of the name and the strength of Yahweh (Mic 5:3–5). He is the child born for Israel, whose name is that of Yahweh himself (Isa 9:6–7).

It is within these dismal conditions of exile and dispersion that God begins to reveal the bright and glorious sunshine of restoration for the people and the land, which will be accomplished by his supernatural power and holy zeal. Micah provides a convenient program to follow (Mic 4:1—5:5, and Mic 7:14–20), while others such as Isaiah and Jeremiah provide more detailed expressions of the purposes of God concerning his people and the land.

In highly figurative language, the prophets declare that the little hill of Zion that housed the temple of God representing his presence, redemption, and rule, will be elevated as the greatest of the mountains of the earth (Isa 2:2; Mic 4:1). It was usual for many pagans to house their gods on natural high places or ziggurats. But God declares that his presence, redemption, and rule will have victorious sway over the world of men and will eclipse and displace the many false gods of men. His service will no longer appear as one of many religions, such as Judaism had at one time appeared to Greco-Roman polytheism.

Essential to this elevation of Mount Zion as chief of the mountains of the earth will be the restoration of the people of Israel as the true and devoted servants of Yahweh, and these will be restored to their land—the land of Israel (Isa 43:1–7; Ezek 34:13; Ezek 36:24; Ezek 37:12, 14). Yahweh will make an "everlasting covenant of peace" with Israel; that is, they will not be allowed again within God's sovereignty to experience the failure of sinful disobedience (Isa 61:8; Isa 63:17), but will always be kept as Yahweh's devoted people through the transformation and sustaining strength of his Holy Spirit (Isa 51:1–3; Isa 54:11–17; Isa 62:1–5; Ezek 37:26; Ezek 39:29; Amos 9:15). Accordingly, Yahweh's sanctuary will be "in their midst forever" (Ezek 37:27–28; Rev 21:3, 22). None of the renewed Israel will be left outside of her homeland (Ezek 39:28). Yahweh will "not hide his face from them any longer" because he will have poured out his Spirit upon the house of Israel (Ezek 39:29).

God will do more than restore Israel to her land; he will greatly increase her inhabitants by a miraculous manner that will amaze her. This increase is probably to be accounted for by the inclusion, not only of the return of the Jews to the biblical service, but of the gentile converts to Yahweh through the salvation provided by Israel's Messiah, who would be the "banner" displayed for the nations (Isa 11:10). God promises the joyful condition that while Jerusalem is desolate from dispersion, she will beget true children more abundantly than when she had her Jewish citizens during her normal inhabitation before dispersion (Isa 54:1). Not only is the increase caused by the greater fruitfulness of newly-begotten sons and daughters during the period of rejected Zion (the "bereaved woman"), more than when Zion was inhabited by Israel (the "married woman" who had produced natural citizens), but also, Israel will "possess the nations" (Isa 49:20–23; Isa 54:1–3; Amos 9:12). The scripture is clear that, at this time, it will be the nations "who are called by his name" that Israel will possess.

God will so bless Israel in the latter days, as a recompense for all the oppressed, deported, and slaughtered Hebrew children that Zion has experienced, by which he will cause an amazing increase of new children as her citizens. And even the gentile nations will bring her Hebrew children back to Zion with respect and sensitivity to their divine calling with which they have been honored (Isa 49:14–26). The gentile nations will have this respect toward the Israelites because they themselves will be made partakers in the grace of the covenant with Abraham that was always intended as a "light to the gentiles," and they will receive the offered salvation and join themselves to the beloved and honored people of God (Isa 49:1, 5–7, 22–23; Isa 60:1–22; Zech 8:20–23).

The restoration of Israel will be accomplished not with the earlier method of appealing to their consciences alone but by the supernatural transformation of the changed heart that only the Spirit of God can effect—the circumcision of the heart that he has promised Israel (Deut 30:6). As surely as water causes vegetative growth, so God's Spirit being poured out on Israel will cause them to be thoroughly repentant and devoted to Yahweh (Isa 44:1–5; Jer 31:7–14, 31–34; Ezek 36:22–36). And as miraculous as the resurrection of the dead, so will be the general return of the Israelites to their true relationship with Yahweh (Ezek 37:1–14). They will rejoice that once they had been under the wrath of God but that now he has had compassion on them (Isa 12:1–6). God will ensure this by his reviving power so that Israel will be the glorious righteous nation among the nations that he has always desired (Isa 60:21; Isa 61:3; Isa 62:1–5; see also Exod 19:3–6; Deut 4:1–8, 20, 32–40). Israel's God will not rest until he has "made Jerusalem a praise in the earth," and that his people are blessed, as the Torah had promised for covenant faithfulness (Isa 62:6–12).

Along with this glorification of the nation of Israel in the world will be the appropriate installation of Yahweh's anointed King with the birth of the Son of Israel given to Israel—the Branch of Jesse, the chosen Servant of Yahweh who we eventually learn is the Messiah Jesus. Yahweh has his prophet designate him as righteous and faithful, having done no violence nor deceit. All the nations' rulers are commanded to honor him (Ps 2:1–9; Isa 11:1–5; Mic 5:2–5). Most significantly, he was to be regarded as Yahweh himself, having his name (Isa 9:6–7; Mic 5:4). He is the second David, whose fallen booth God has promised to raise up again (Amos 9:11). He is the one king over the reunited houses of Judah and Israel as "one stick" (Ezek 37:15–28).

What is also amazing and essential to the elevation of God's holy hill is the global ingathering of the gentile nations to lay hold of the revelation, the redemption, and the service of Yahweh (Isa 2:3; Zech 8:20–23). This must be part of the actual process through which this tremendous event of the ascendancy of the true religion of Yahweh is brought about. The prophesied Davidic ruler, the anointed Servant of Yahweh, is clearly described as bringing the knowledge and salvation of Yahweh to the gentile nations (Isa 9:6–7; Isa 11:1–5; Isa 42:1–4; Isa 49:1–7; Mic 5:2–5). This Messiah would be divinely commissioned not only as the savior of the Israelites but also as a banner for the nations who will flee to him and will find glorious rest in his place (Isa 11:10; Mic 5:5). It will be the time to gather all nations and tongues, who will come and see Yahweh's glory (Isa 66:18) באה לקבץ את־כל־הגוים והלשנות ובאו וראו את־כבודי.

With the supernatural exaltation of Zion the gentile nations will stream to her, desiring to know God and his word (Isa 2:2–3; Mic 4:1–2). The nations will come to see the profound value of knowing the true God and will seek him and entreat his favor בירושלם ולחלות את־פני יהוה ובאו עמים רבים וגוים עצומים לבקש את־יהוה צבאות (Zech 8:22). The redeemed Jews will be honored in that the gentiles will recognize that they know the true God and desire to join them. They will know that there is only salvation and peace, righteousness and strength, in drawing near to him in Zion (Isa 45:14–17, 22–25; Isa 49:22–23; Isa 60:3; Zech 8:20–23). It is clear that the time that the prophesied Messiah, the righteous Branch of Jesse, was to be born to become the ruler over Israel was also the beginning of the time to gather all nations and tongues (Isa 11:10). Not only will they be drawn to the living God's glory but some will be sent as missionaries to yet other gentiles to declare his glory to them (Isa 66:19). In some sense, undoubtedly because of the exaltation of Zion and the compassion of God, the gentile nations will even carry the Jews back to her and serve them according to the contribution of their own national glory with true conviction of the priority of the Hebrews' holy calling (Isa 60:4–14; Isa 66:20).

What is also clearly revealed by the prophets is that the general ingathering of the gentiles is certainly connected to, and inaugurated by, the commission of the chosen Servant of Yahweh. This commission will consist of a divinely anointed *preaching* ministry that effects the conversion of the humble and the judgment of the wicked (Isa 42:1–7; Isa 49:1–6; Isa 52:13–15; Isa 61:1–3). His prophetic ministry would also be combined with the priestly role of offering up the sacrifice of himself as a guilt offering for the atonement of his people who obey him (Isa 50:4, 10; Isa 53:10–12).

It seems clear from both careful consideration of these amazing things promised through the prophets, and the humble observation of actual historical providence, that of the gradual realization and growth of these spiritual experiences among both Jews and gentiles who believe on the Messiah Jesus, and of the reacquisition of the land of Israel, that these purposes of God are now being only partially realized but will somehow consummate according to the full extent pictured by the absolute prophecies of scripture.

What is very important to bear in mind when interpreting these prophecies of Israel's future glory and restoration is that God is speaking, not of rabbinic Jews or mere ethnic Jews, but of those Hebrews who have come to see the truth that the prophesied Messiah has come and has inaugurated the New Covenant. They are the ones who believe in, trust in, and obey the Servant of Yahweh who bore the punishment of their sins. They are the ones who understand that they must be connected to the Messiah through faith and love because he was given by God as a covenant to the people. That is, in him all the covenants are fulfilled with all the righteousness and devotion that Yahweh required.

Therefore, these promises cannot have been realized in the post-exilic conditions of the Jewish returnees from Babylon since it can be seen both scripturally and historically that there were yet evidences of imperfect obedience and sinful behavior of the general populace of returnees, which is patently inconsistent with the glorious descriptions above. In fact, many of the exiled Jews did not wish to return to Jerusalem because they were comfortable in their foreign social-economic circumstances, and so proved that their heart was not bent toward the glory of God as prescribed by the call of the Mosaic covenant. They were not really interested in living as a truly sanctified people in their sanctified land.

When the Judeans were actually delivered from their Babylonian captivity, Yahweh had commanded these delivered ones to resume their holy and separated calling as the special people of God (Isa 52:11). But many refused. This reprehensible characterization can be seen during the prophetic records that reflect the post-exilic period of conditions among the Jewish returnees to Jerusalem, such as Nehemiah, Haggai, and Malachi, which have many indictments and even curses for sinful disobedience.

The correct interpretation of these significant eschatological prophecies depends entirely upon two important controlling elements: As this book has emphasized, without the sovereign initiative of the Holy Spirit changing the heart, there will never be a faith or love that is biblically demanded that would ensure the correct spiritual evaluation of biblical concerns, such as the sinful nature and the means of reconciliation with God for either Jew or gentile. And then there must be a careful regard for all of the passages of prophetic disclosure that are germane to these eschatological concepts.

The interpretations of rabbinic Judaism fail to appreciate the spiritual nature of the prophecies, precisely because they prove to not have the Spirit in that they interpret the scriptures according to the distorted view of their invented Judaism. If their view of God is invented, their interpretations cannot but fail to be erroneous. This substitute religion only understands life according to an unchanged heart, and consequently only understands spiritual influence according to the ability of an external message to impact the conscience—much like the early Israelites were impacted by the disclosures of Yahweh through the ministry of Moses.

It is only a fleshly, earthly, material influence that appeals to man's human commonality and common worldly desires while they remain unchanged in their spirit's fundamental attitude toward God. It yet remains that their impulse to serve God comes from without, from fleshly and material advantages (such as social-economic prosperity) and not from within, implanted by the Spirit of God, where one cannot help but love God because of his worthiness that is unaffected by outward circumstances.

The result is interpretations that focus on normally experienced political influence, such as the depiction of the nations being persuaded to defer to the king and nation of Israel for mere political arbitration and social justice. But just as surely as early Israel was required by Yahweh to circumcise their heart but in the end Yahweh must promise to perform this heart-circumcision himself, so today and in the future, the ideal Messianic age will not be brought about by the worldly, material influence of rabbinic Judaism's message of moral reform and social justice, nor their impoverished effort toward *tikkun olam*.

Rather, the blessings of the Messianic age, which we believe has begun with the appearance of the Messiah Jesus, will be brought about by the attending power of the Holy Spirit transforming the deeper nature of individual men and women to turn wholeheartedly to the God of Abraham, Isaac, and Jacob. This conversion will be according to the strict and demanding biblical conditions of contrition before God for sin (Isa 57:15; Isa 66:2), freely confessing God as the only source of righteousness and strength (Isa 45:22–25), the glad binding of oneself to God to love his name (Isa 56:6), seeking and delighting in God's revealed word (Isa 2:3; Zech 8:21–22), and obedience to the prophets' revelation of redemption—including trusting in the atonement of the Messiah Jesus (Isa 50:10; Isa 52:13—53:12).

It will be brought about by the experience of one individual after another being implanted with the impulse for love to God that then comes from within, along with the attending love that each individual will have toward his fellow godly person. The Kingdom of the Messiah will spread with the increase of such conversions globally, contributing to the prophetic depictions found in scripture concerning the restoration of Israel as a whole and the turning of the gentiles to Israel's God.

18

The Grace of Spiritual Sonship

IN OUR FALLEN WORLD, there is the popular notion that all men are, in fact, "the children of God" by virtue, at the very least, of their having been created by him. It is also sustained by a vague perception that the Creator must be good and so, therefore, he must love, in an approving sense, all men. But this is a serious mistake due to ignorance of the actual message of the Bible and fallen mankind's true nature. The reality, according to the scriptures, is that *all men are estranged from God* because of the sinful nature, and consequently have no positive relationship with him. They neither know him nor seek him in truth according to the scriptures. They assume they are already accepted by him due to their being created by him and their *mistaken opinions of acceptable moral character.* The Bible teaches a very different cause for someone to be regarded a child of God.

Beginning with the sacred scroll of the Torah, and carried forward with the later prophets, there are several metaphorical terms or pictures to describe the people of God as really belonging to Yahweh, through the grace of redemption. Such designations include the collective people of Israel being regarded the "wife" of Yahweh her "husband" (Isa 54:5), or the "son" of Yahweh (Exod 4:22), or they are "his sons and daughters" (Isa 43:6), and he is their "Father" (Isa 63:16). But the designation of "sons" or "daughters" is perhaps the dear and prominent usage, not least because it may be applied directly to each individual believer. We read that Yahweh first calls his collectively- and externally-redeemed people his "son" to Pharaoh (Exod 4:23). But it is during the ominous song of indictment that Moses further describes Yahweh as the Rock who "begot" them, or, the God who "gave them birth" (Deut 32:18; see Isa 44:1–2, 21, 24).

The essential idea in these designations of the begetting of a son for the collective people of Israel is used, during the career of Moses, to indicate the fact that God has produced this people by his design and grace rather than their own initiative. He has formed them to be his special possession by his own initiative and not their own doing. He "gave them birth" by his favor (Deut 32:6–14), and they are graciously regarded as the "sons of the Lord" (Deut 14:1). And this essential idea of the divine initiative in producing a people for his glory is stressed concisely in the prophets (Isa 43:6–7).

These designations found in the Torah, however, are also used in a delimited sense congruent with the external call during the wilderness period when Yahweh took the people "by the hand" to be in covenant with him, since he denounces the sinful people as proving to be "not his children" because of their persistent corruption, and mentions the provocation of "his sons and daughters" (Deut 32:5, 18–20). Then, in a special sense, during the united monarchy of Israel when God was about to establish a special covenant with David and his house, God designated the anointed ruler as his "son" (2 Sam 7:14–15). In this case, it meant one of the Davidic kings that was especially loved by divine adoption—which is considered a "begetting" (Ps 2:1–12). Nevertheless, the type is very fitting and meaningful in that it conveys two correct ideas:

1. The complete non-involvement of a people's will concerning the beginning of their life as separated unto God's service (as was the case with the nation of Israel), or an individual person being made spiritually alive to God (as is the case for those who are born again), even as a natural baby has no say whatsoever regarding the eventuation of its birth.

2. The normal experience of the love and care of a parent for his own child.

So then, the idea in this type used by Moses is precious and a favored one with the inspired writers of later scripture and points up the fact that if there is ever to be a people that will truly belong to God, they will be *produced by his sovereign initiative,* which involves his separating them from the sinful mass of the world through the supernatural work of the Spirit on their hearts. God will not be disgraced but will yet be glorified by making for himself a people that truly love him and keep his covenant (Jer 32:37–41).

Regarding the external call of ancient Israel, this type truly indicated the divine initiative in Yahweh's forming a people for himself when he delivered them from Egypt; and regarding the internal call, by the Spirit's work according to the New Covenant with a later generation in days to come, it indicates more profoundly the grace of the divine initiative in forming a people who will keep covenant by clinging to Yahweh forever. So, when it comes about that God discloses that he will put forth his Spirit to produce many people that will love him from a renewed heart, Isaiah designates these as "children" and "sons" (Isa 43:6–7; Isa 49:14–21; Isa 54:1–3).

This metaphor of "children," and "sons," and "sons and daughters" is picked up as a favored expression of the grace of God by both the Messiah Jesus and several Jewish writers of the New Testament; it is the true designation of those who are given a second, spiritual "birth" that results in a new spiritual life toward God (Matt 5:9, 45; Luke 6:35; Rom 8:14, 16; 2 Cor 6:16–18; Gal 3:26; Gal 4:5–7; Jas 1:18).

It is the frequent expression of John, who most clearly teaches the absolute sovereignty and invaluable grace involved in the granting of this experience (John 1:12–13; 1 John 3:1–2, 9–10; 1 John 4:7; 1 John 5:4). John is very clear that only those individuals who actually do receive the Messiah Jesus are the ones who are given the right to be regarded as the children of God, and he emphasizes that these are not begotten by their own human choice but by God's will alone. The genuine children of God are those "who were born not of blood, nor of the will of the flesh, nor of the will of man, but of God" οι ουκ εξ αιματων ουδε εκ θεληματος σαρκος ουδε εκ θεληματος ανδρος αλλ εκ θεου εγεννηθησαν (John 1:13). That is, they have received the Messiah Jesus because God had already performed the secret work of giving them new spiritual birth (John 1:12–13; John 3:5–8).

The *new birth* is necessary in order to begin to appreciate the message of Jesus and the true nature of the Kingdom of God; otherwise, if one is not born again, he cannot "see" or "enter" the Kingdom of God εαν μη τις γεννηθη ανωθεν ου δυναται ιδειν την βασιλειαν του θεου (John 3:3, 5). This metaphor of a second- or heavenly-produced "birth" γεννηθη ανωθεν probably derives from the Torah's expressions regarding the formation of Israel as the people of God as his "son" whom he "begot" (Exod 4:22; Deut 32:6, 18; see Isa 44:2, 24), since Jesus reminds Nicodemus that this is a teaching based in the Law of Israel (John 3:9–12). This new birth is sheer lavishing of grace and one of the sweetest acts of God toward those whom he has set his love upon from before the foundation of the world, that the holy God would make us his own beloved children by his transforming grace and adopt our sinful persons (Eph 1:3–8).

Let there be no mistake that it is the consistent and unified teaching of the Torah, the Prophets, and the Messiah Jesus, that Yahweh regards no one as his true spiritual child except those who are begotten by his sovereign initiative and who prove it by obedience to his word (Deut 32:5–6; John 8:31–47). This unity proves evangelical knowledge.

19

The Sovereignty of Divine Grace

IN ORDER TO EFFECTIVELY discuss that distinctive characteristic of the grace of God toward mankind—the divine selectivity involved in its dispensation—and to urge its truthfulness as a biblical revelation, it is best to once again rehearse biblical salvation history. But this time, we will pay special attention to the divine abandonment. The facts of *omission* must not be overlooked in our study of the divine redemption, if we are to grasp the fullness of God's saving activities.

Now, it has been previously shown that from the very first of the inscripturated revelations of God and throughout the development of the writings of the Hebrew prophets, that mankind is wholly and continually sinful, and that this involves both the pursuit of evil and the inability to change (Gen 6:5; Ps 14:2–3; Isa 59:7–8; Jer 4:22; Jer 13:23; Jer 17:9). This unquestionable biblical doctrine must be understood and borne in mind, in order to taste the sweetness of God's grace toward the elect. Its truth forms the very black backdrop against which God's bright flashes of kindness are made to appear in various lives.

When the foregoing earlier discussion of the actual sinful condition of mankind is thoroughly understood, there then should be felt a profound despair; there then should be seen the absolute inability of anyone, whether Jew or gentile, to deliver himself from this spiritual prison. In fact, it is of the horrible nature of this prison that no one will care to emerge from it in order to be able to stand before our holy God with acceptance.

Such callousness of the Hebrews that is depicted by the prophets must also be said of the gentiles since they share the same sinful nature. When Yahweh determined to call and invite the chosen race to be in covenant with him and know him in a redemptive sense, their spirit was found to be uncaring and insensitive to their spiritual need; they did not seek Yahweh by their own initiative (Isa 65:1). But Israel's indifference is only noticed because of God's focused attention toward them. The same evil character can be assumed for any other nation, because "There is none who seeks for God" (Rom 3:11). With our God, however, is the mystery of pure love that will care to rescue wretched man from this misery by the working of supernatural power; and this pure love resides as an essential characteristic of the interior of God's sublime being. But along with this divine blessedness is the attribute of sovereignty: power and purposes *answerable to no one and influenced by no condition.*

In the wilderness, after Israel had been freed from Egypt through Moses and led to the holy mountain, where God continued to meet with Moses to give them their distinctive code of ethics, and the people had shamefully proved unfaithful, Moses was willing to mediate for them and was earnestly pleading for their pardon. God indeed was moved to relent of his intention to destroy the people for their idolatrous defection (Exod 32:1–14).

Then Moses became especially desirous to know God's presence, intention, and glory concerning his dealings with the people. It is then that God takes the opportunity to emphatically disclose his glory to Moses, which involves the basic nature of his saving activity with mankind (which has actually been demonstrated since his gracious relationship with the Semitic race). His glory involves that his saving activities—the granting of grace and mercy—would be based only on his *selective determinations.* He will be gracious to whom he will be gracious, and have compassion on whom he will have compassion (Exod 33:12–19).

Important implications should be noticed here in these significant Pentateuchal passages that we have been examining. The saving response from man of repentance from sin and loving attachment to God that he commands will indeed be effected, not by waiting upon their inability, but by an operation within them that must come from outside of themselves. "Circumcision" is a metaphor that God uses to emphasize that; just as the literal rite of circumcision removes what is ordinarily found with man's nature, so also he will effectively remove what is ordinarily found within the chosen man's heart: the propensity to hate God and love evil.

Moreover, if God says he will do this, then it cannot be done by a man's own native ability, because *an evil heart cannot throw off an evil heart.* But as always with God's dealings with man, he is sovereign in his determinations to save and bless because he has forever declared that he will be gracious to whom he will be gracious, and he will be compassionate to whom he will be compassionate (Exod 33:19).

When we read the sacred accounts of God's saving and gracious interaction with men, we see that God was always the one *to initiate a relationship* that will involve grace and lovingkindness. Consider the examples of Adam, Noah, Abraham, Isaac, Jacob, as discussed above. Then with the redemption of Israel from Egypt through the service of Moses and Aaron, they are made to follow God's leadings and are brought to the holy mountain in the Sinai and commanded to enter into covenant with their God who has bought them so mercifully. They are commanded to enter into this covenant *really without a choice,* for to refuse was to be "cut off"—they would be destroyed. This covenant arrangement was not requested by the people but was the initiative of his sovereignty. It was surely good and for their good, that they might live and be loved; but it was not their idea, it was God's initiating grace.

There is an important correlative aspect to these redemptive events that is rather overlooked by many teachers of the Bible: when God decided to redeem Israel and take her for a people as his own possession, he also *decided not to take any of the other nations surrounding Israel.* This aspect is logically and philosophically necessary. It is both an undeniable fact and plainly declared in scripture. Moses and the people of Israel were conscious of this redemptive separation (Exod 33:16). This is one of the many important and momentous ways that God demonstrates his sovereignty in all his dealings with his world.

From the impenetrable mind of God alone come the reasons, and the good pleasure of his will and purposes, of which we never learn. The very motivations as to why the choice of this individual and not that individual, this nation and not that nation, this eventuation and not that eventuation, comes to pass is never really disclosed to us in the Bible. But we are told to respect this majestic sovereignty, for "the secret things belong to the Lord our God, but the things revealed belong to us" (Deut 29:29).

So then, when we come to the New Testament, we see the Messiah Jesus declaring similarly the manner in which God the Father will be glorified in his redeemed people. He is glorified in their sanctity and their special love for one another. It will be this evidence before the unbelievers that will bring glory to God for his grace toward them. This grace is regarded as selectively granted in contradistinction to the unbelieving "world" around them (Matt 5:16; John 17:6–23; Jas 1:18; 1 Pet 2:9–10; Rev 3:9).

In fact, the very principle that had operated within God's sovereign determinations, with regard to his calling and sanctifying the Hebrew Patriarchs and their offspring, is manifested in the era of gentile salvation. The Jewish writers of the New Testament are persuaded by the Holy Spirit that the grace being given to the gentiles, along with the Jews being called to salvation, is motivated by the same principle that God will be glorified through their selective salvation; and that they, wherever they are found, *collectively constitute the real chosen race* made holy for his own possession in the world (Eph 1:3–14; Eph 2:11–22; 1 Pet 2:9–10).

In order to be clear about this matter of God being glorified by the taking of a portion of mankind for his own people who will love and fear him, we must carefully consider many Bible passages that evince the negative aspect of this solemn fact. These are verses that contain the unashamed statements of God, declared by himself or through the medium of his prophets, concerning the divine intentions to delimit his redemptive work toward mankind, whether Jew or gentile. Again, these are verses which are rather poorly understood, or are willfully misunderstood, or are eviscerated and made to say something quite different than what was originally intended.

As salvation history is traced and contemplated, beginning with Israel's Torah, it must be honestly seen that, both in God's dealings and in certain declarations, he has *not been willing to redeem every individual person on earth.* We have seen that God chose to encounter certain persons and not multitudes of others that he might have had dealings with. He chose to bless Abram and not his brothers Nahor and Haran. He chose to bless Jacob and not Esau. It must be admitted that all the while these were being blessed with a real relationship with the living God, many thousands of other peoples were being left to their darkness and estrangement. Nor were these redeemed individuals honored with a vital relationship with God because they supposedly sought after this blessed relationship, because it is denied due to the fact of the biblical declaration that "no one seeks after God" in the hardness of their unchanged heart (Gen 6:5; Ps 14:1–3).

A prominent example, which serves also as a type, of the sovereignty of electing love (and the implied rejection of others) is the *choice of Israel* to be the nation brought into a right relationship with God. God unashamedly declares that Israel was separated to be his own people; that they were not chosen because they were the most numerous as though abundance of souls compelled his determinations, for they were the fewest; that they were loved because of his prior covenant with their fathers and not merely because of their own needs; that God's decision in taking them from among other nations resulted in his choosing to leave those others to their darkness and sin, even destroying them for the sake of his purposes with his own people (Deut 4:32–38; Deut 7:6–8; Isa 43:3–4).

The election of the Hebrews in the nation of Israel is to be regarded, even as God himself regards it, as an eminent means by which God gains glory and the fear that is due him. Moreover, this principle of God taking a portion of humanity for his own possession, for his glory, will always be the manner of his sovereign dealings both in the election of the nation of Israel, and of various remnants within the nations of Israel and Judah, and finally with the various Jewish and gentile individuals throughout history (Deut 4:6–8, 32–38; Deut 9:4–6; Ps 33:12; Ps 67:1–7; Isa 49:1, 6; Isa 51:4–5; Zech 8:20–23).

But then even within the nation of Israel, the Torah reveals that God was dealing sovereignly with the individuals who comprised that people. As we have seen in our discussion above, this fact is important to discern especially for the Jews, as it is their special history, since they have always been persuaded by their sages to think of their race as ordinarily close and faithful to God's covenant *en masse*.

This ominous fact of Bible revelation cannot be denied, though we may feel it is horrifying to consider. It cannot be honestly denied that God has willed to be glorified for his saving grace through the separation of the Israelites from the rest of the nations (Deut 7:6; Ps 147:19–20), through the election of a remnant of Israel from the rest of that nation at various times (1 Kgs 19:18; Ps 4:3; Isa 6:8–13), through the predestination of some individuals to salvation while the rest are destined to damnation (Rom 9:18; 1 Thess 5:9), through his willingness to demonstrate his wrath toward those "vessels of wrath prepared for destruction" while he "makes known the riches of his glory upon vessels of mercy" (Rom 9:22–23). We who have been redeemed can only bow down in profound gratitude, and shed even endless tears of joy.

Special Love Given to the Elect Believers

IF A REDEEMED PERSON, whether a Jewish believer or a gentile believer in the Messiah Jesus, is to fully appreciate the grace that God has shown toward him, then he must be aware of the *electing love* of God recorded in the salvation history of the Bible. As we have seen earlier in the discussion of the profound revelations of the Torah, the first acts of grace for the purposes of redemption were sovereign initiatives toward certain individuals in the Patriarchal history; such as Abel, Enoch, Noah, and especially Abraham, Isaac, and Jacob (Gen 5:22, 24; Gen 6:8; Gen 12:1–3; Gen 21:1–3; Gen 26:1–6; Gen 28:10–17; Josh 24:2–3). These did not seek out God's favor first but were made to receive it unasked. And if we believe and bear in mind the biblical context of the revealed doctrine of the general sinfulness of mankind and consequent spiritual deadness toward the Creator (Gen 6:5), then we know that these favored ones of Patriarchal history were not found to be meritorious in character before God brought them near to him in his saving activity.

Eventually, according to his covenantal fidelity toward the Hebrew Patriarchs, God resolved to rescue and redeem the Hebrew slaves from Egyptian bondage and to make them his specially formed nation who would worship and serve him alone (Gen 12:2; Gen 15:12–21; Gen 17:2; Gen 22:17; Gen 26:4). Their only possible claim on the compassion of God was not their righteousness but the previously granted Covenant of Grace and its concomitant promises of blessing and land, given to Abraham, Isaac, and Jacob (Exod 2:24; Deut 9:4–6; Isa 41:8). It is expressly for this divine arrangement, based upon the *unmerited love that he set upon* Abraham, that God took an interest in the Hebrews to form a special relationship with them (Deut 7:6–8). Accordingly, it was to the sons of Israel that God gave the priceless scriptures and his holy laws which rendered them a unique and highly favored people in the midst of a very dark and perverse world of heathens (Gen 18:16–19; Exod 19:5; Deut 4:5–8, 32–40; Deut 7:6; Deut 33:2–5; Ps 147:19–20; Amos 3:2).

After the establishment of the nation of Israel and her settlement in the land of Canaan, when there is to be seen continual provocations and general infidelity toward God (1 Sam 8:8; Ps 5:8–10; Isa 48:1–8; Isa 66:5; Dan 9:6), there are the recorded lives of divinely elected individuals who served God as judges, prophets, and kings and, undoubtedly, other small portions of the populace of the nation who pursued godliness with genuine faith and love. These are made to stand out as different in their spirits, loving and clinging to God and his word, while the outwardly religious and spiritually dead brethren hated them, or oppressed them, and excluded them from their hypocritical society. They were different than their formal, rebellious, syncretistic brethren around them. Some notable examples are to be found in the psalms (Ps 4:3; Ps 31:9–13, 18; Ps 35:11–26; Ps 36:1–4, 10–12; Ps 41:4–9; Ps 50:16–21; Ps 55:12–15; Ps 69:7–12, 20–28).

And so, even within the foundational revelation of the Torah we see that redemption from sin was given to individuals whom God elected to love, but eventually he purposed to form a nation of his worshipers but that failed because the vast majority were not given special love. Then ultimately, God revealed that he will do the new thing of making a new covenant that displaces the failed experiment of the national covenant. This new covenant will consist only of those individuals who have been changed in their spirits to truly love God, whether that individual is Jewish or gentile. This new covenant will also be the unveiling of the *age of gentile inclusion* into the Hebrew community of Yahweh's servants (Rom 16:25–26; Gal 3:8–9, 14; Eph 3:1–6; Col 1:26–27).

The consistent revelation of scripture throughout all epochs of salvation history is that *God wills to be glorified by the separation of a portion of people from fallen humanity for his service.* He purposes to be loved for his grace in the lives of those few who are favored in God's sovereignty. He designs to make a difference in those spirits that he changes in order *to be seen as the only source of thoroughgoing holiness and pure love in the world.* This fact is evident from the initial interactions recounted in the Torah: such as Enoch who walked with God, or righteous Noah who by his commission "condemned the world" (Heb 11:7), or the separating calls of Abraham, Isaac, and Jacob, or the proven devotion of Joseph,

Joshua, and Caleb. With the calling of the nation of Israel, God was supposed to be glorified by the sanctified character of the people, and which were intentionally separated out the rest of humanity and made to be seen as different and loved by the God of heaven and earth (Deut 4:6–8, 32–34; Deut 7:6; Ps 147:19–20; Isa 41:8–9; Isa 43:10–13; Amos 3:2).

Accordingly, we see that the Messiah Jesus and his ambassadors continue the teaching of the Hebrew Bible concerning the same intention of God to be glorified in the salvation of relatively few persons and not the whole world. Jesus came specifically for "the lost sheep of the house of Israel" and not the gentile "dogs" (Matt 15:21–28; see Matt 10:5–6). It was the evident conviction and the consistent teaching of the Apostle Paul that the Hebrew Bible reveals the critical truth of God's sovereign intention to save elect individuals by the grace of granted love toward them alone. Paul constantly contrasts the state of sinful mankind being unsaved by God with the blessedness of those *who are being saved* from sin and darkness through the selective granting of redeeming grace (Rom 9:22–26; 1 Cor 1:18–31; Eph 2:1–10; 2 Thess 2:11–14; Titus 3:3–7). And it is especially through the Johannine corpus of inspired writings that we hear the most emphatic declarations of this divine intention to be glorified in the small body of genuine disciples, walking differently from humanity around them, being blessed with the true fellowship of God (John 3:21; John 17:9–10, 22–23).

In pursuing this sovereign purpose of being glorified by a special people who truly serve him, God brings about this situation by giving the *greatest kind of love* to elect individuals, which is the kindness of actual rescuing help in turning their hearts toward him. As we have seen abundantly in our study of the Torah and the development of the later prophets, God determines to change a person by supernatural power so that he is *definitively rescued* from divine wrath and judgment. That person will certainly embrace the offered salvation, trusting in the atoning death and resurrection of the Messiah Jesus, as we have learned from the prophets, and will become a child of God in spirit and truth.

In love, God does not wait for our inability, but overlooks our demerit and proceeds to alter our spirits to lovingly respond to his offer of salvation and to walk accordingly to his call to holiness and love (1 John 2:29; see Rom 5:6, 8, 10; Eph 1:4). And so it is by *special love* that God causes those who are the called to love him, and does not pass over them his actual redemption. In special love, he produces faith and love in their heart and adopts them as his own children (Eph 1:5; 1 Tim 1:14; 1 John 5:4). With special love, he loved the elect persons first so that they then are able to love him in return as well as those others who belong to him (1 John 3:14, 23; 1 John 4:7, 19; 1 John 5:1). This is the most important kind of love that God gives to man, which does not merely offer salvation but actually brings it about in individual lives (1 John 3:1). And so it is by this principle of distinctive affection, for both God and fellow believers, that the real people of God will appear different to the sinful world around them and bring glory to the living God.

The famous verse in the fourth gospel (John 3:16), which declares the love of God for the world by his giving his son for the sinners' salvation, is a poorly interpreted verse in the popular understanding, including many teachers of the Bible who should know better. In this passage when Jesus (or perhaps the narrator of the fourth gospel) states that "God so loved the world, etc.," it is usually understood as proclaiming the *magnitude* of God's love for sinful mankind. It is as though the amount of this love was pressuring the heart of God to induce the giving of his son, in an effort to go through any expense to attract the return of the sinful world back to him.

Despite the warmth of this popular reading, neither the foundational teaching of the Torah, nor the later understanding of the prophets, nor the Hebraic background, nor the context of the passage, nor the sense of the Greek language, will support it. The Messiah Jesus provides the correct understanding, referring to the account in the Torah of the rebellious Israelites in the wilderness who were bitten by fiery snakes for their irreverence toward Yahweh (Num 21:4–9). The determined compassion of Yahweh, induced by Moses' intercession, was conditioned with the stipulation that those afflicted were to look at a bronze serpent lifted up on a stick by Moses. Those among the bitten ones who happened to believe in this divine remedy so as to look at the serpent image were healed and spared. Though Yahweh was enraged with these rebellious ones, what he offered was that kind of love called mercy, and the mercy offered was conditioned upon belief in the remedy offered. Whether all the bitten ones had this necessary faith in the terms, that is, the *manner* ουτως of receiving forgiveness that Yahweh had set forth is not stated; and so perhaps not all were spared God's wrath due to disbelief in the divinely stipulated remedy of the bronze serpent. The point is that sovereign terms were required for the offered mercy. When a man "looked to the bronze serpent, he lived" (Num 21:9).

Accordingly, Jesus asserted that it is in "this manner" ουτως in which God would grant mercy to sinners. The offer is specifically that if the sinful world would believe the terms that God has sovereignly extended to it, that of loving attachment and reliance on the Sent One and his atoning death and resurrection, then they would be given eternal life. Jesus is declaring the sovereign terms of salvation from sin to the fallen world; that is, the manner in which God's grace will be obtained. It is *the divine love in the offer of eternal life to an undeserving world* that is being stated here in this passage, not the magnitude or the greatest kind of love for the world. Supporting this, we have seen already in our study of the Torah and its development by the later prophets that God does not love the world so much, or in such a manner, so as to certainly rescue by his power every individual that has lived. That great magnitude of divine love, popularly imagined here to be for all the world, is really only had by, or given to, those chosen to be rescued by transforming grace by which they are certainly made children of God (John 10:25–30; John 15:16; John 17:22–24; Eph 1:3–6; 1 Pet 1:1–5; 1 John 3:1).

God has determined to set his love upon, and powerfully redeem for himself, individuals from the nation of Israel and also from every ethnic group throughout the world; and they are those who now, under the New Covenant, collectively constitute the "chosen nation" for his own glorious and loving possession (Gal 3:8, 14, 28–29; 1 Pet 2:9–10; Rev 5:9–10). Nevertheless, there is considerable love in the form of undeserved mercy in the offer of salvation given in this proclamation. The context brings this correct understanding into focus because the next verse stresses the kindness of God in sending his son into the world not for the purpose of condemning the world, which it certainly deserved, but to provide a means of salvation for it (John 3:17). But it is offered, not granted.

God is offering a means of salvation and reconciliation to a lost and sinful world, to the Jew first but also to the gentile (Rom 1:16), when in truth he was under no obligation to do so. From the subjective standpoint, God will indeed give eternal life *to those who do respond* in faith to his message. He will forgive sin and give his Fatherly love to those who do turn their hearts to him (John 14:21, 23). That this salvation is made available and freely received, upon repentance from a life of sin, to anyone *who realizes that he must have it* is the kind of love declared in this particular passage. We must keep in mind the controlling context of the entire passage to appreciate this correct reading. The sense is conditioned by the Torah account of the bronze serpent, where God is enraged and ready to kill those offensive ones, but instead offers a chance at pardon. The sense is also conditioned by the fact stated at the end of the present passage (John 3:36), that the offensive world, while being offered a chance at salvation, remains under the wrath of God. Yahweh does not have warm affection for those deserving his wrath.

To be offered salvation is one thing, but to be *actually saved* is another thing. To hear the message of salvation from the guilt and punishment of sin is God's kindness indeed, but to be *made to believe* the message and receive it is the greater kindness. It is this latter kind of love that God gives to him whom he sets his personal love upon in order to make him a believing child.

When the Apostle Peter writes that the Lord is patiently forbearing his return because he is not willing that any should perish, but that all would come to repentance, he means the Lord is patient toward *the beloved ones* ("toward us" εἰς ἡμᾶς) who have *received the precious gift of faith* that he has in mind (2 Pet 3:9; see 2 Pet 1:1; 2 Pet 3:1, 8, 14–15). The Apostle John teaches that when God causes a man to not only hear the offer of salvation but also to believe in the Messiah Jesus and surrender his heart to his Lordship through the miracle of spiritual birth, then that man has been *given God's intimate love*. He exults in that this is "the great kind of love that God has bestowed on us" (1 John 3:1).

Again, in the Apostle Paul's words, when God changes a person from being indifferent to him to being profoundly sensitive to the things of God, then that person has been given great love (Eph 2:4–5). This precious saving love, which is not given to everyone, has been poured out within our hearts who believe, richly through the giving of the Holy Spirit (Rom 5:5; Titus 3:5–6). It is this greatest, special, differentiating love that makes us strange, and hated, to the world (John 15:19; 1 John 3:1).

134